Discover Creativity with 2–5 Year Olds

Discover Creativity with 2–5 Year Olds explores young children's creative development and shares important insight as to why and how practitioners can encourage their natural curiosity. It will help early years practitioners and professionals to rediscover the joy of working creatively with young children and how to support them in developing their ideas, thoughts and feelings through creative expression and opportunities.

The book provides an in-depth account of what creativity is and how best to support children in their creative endeavours. Covering the prime areas of the early years foundation stage, it is packed with engaging, cost-effective and achievable activity ideas to support the young creative mind. Including case studies, discussion boxes and reflective points, the chapters consider key topics underpinned by theoretical perspectives including the following:

■ Understanding the unique differences and needs of toddlers and pre-school children

■ Forming respectful relationships and understanding the impact they can have on creativity

■ Developing the environment and resources that enable creativity

■ Exploring outdoors and making the most of time with young children outside

■ Encouraging a process over product mindset

■ Understanding the role of the adult in supporting creative thinking and exploration

This wonderful guide will inspire practitioners and equip them with the tools they need to fully support and cultivate the curious and creative side to every child.

Louise Day is an early years graduate, manager of Wally's Day Nursery, UK, and Author of *Discover Creativity with Babies*.

Discover Creativity with 2–5 Year Olds

Promoting Creative Learning and Development Through Best Practice

Louise Day

Routledge
Taylor & Francis Group

LONDON AND NEW YORK

Designed cover image: © Louise Day

First edition published 2023
by Routledge
4 Park Square, Milton Park, Abingdon, Oxon, OX14 4RN

and by Routledge
605 Third Avenue, New York, NY 10158

Routledge is an imprint of the Taylor & Francis Group, an informa business

© 2023 Louise Day

British Library Cataloguing-in-Publication Data
A catalogue record for this book is available from the British Library

ISBN: 978-1-032-22237-0 (hbk)
ISBN: 978-1-032-22235-6 (pbk)
ISBN: 978-1-003-27171-0 (ebk)

DOI: 10.4324/9781003271710

Typeset in Bembo
by Apex CoVantage, LLC

Contents

About the author

Discover Creativity is a series of books that will explore the development of creativity in young children from birth to 5 years. It will explore some of the definitions of creativity as well as some common misconceptions and look at why it matters to children in their earliest years as well as what early years practitioners can do to support children in their creative endeavours. There is a focus within the books on the relationships that children have with those around them and how these relationships and the interactions within them, have a lasting impact on children and their ability to think creatively. Each book will look closely at the environments that are conducive to creativity and how we can foster creative thinking in our settings as well as provide inspiration for those working closely with young children.

The first book in the series, *Discover Creativity with Babies*, looks specifically at babies up to the age of 2. It explores early milestones, crucial attachments and the development of creativity and how this can be fostered and encouraged in early years settings. The second book, *Discover Creativity with 2–5 Year Olds*, follows a similar trajectory, looking further into the idea of creativity, the relationships that children form in their pre-school years and how these play an important role in the development of agency with children aged between 2 and 5 years old (typically before they start primary school in the UK).

The series is the work of Louise Day, an Early Childhood graduate who has spent her career so far working within her family-owned childcare setting to ensure that the children in their care get the best-quality experiences and opportunities. From a young age, her love of the arts and her creative talent meant she had the opportunity to study and exhibit her own work throughout her college years. Combining her love of art, mixed media and early years, after studying for her master's degree, she now spends her days exploring and learning alongside children, sharing with them the joy of creating, giving them the opportunity to explore freely exercise their autonomy, and giving them ownership of their work with annual exhibitions for parents and carers. The series is based primarily on her interest in the development of creativity but also the impact it can have in later childhood and beyond if children have not been allowed to develop their own ideas about what creativity should be or what it looks like through mindful provocations and discoveries.

Acknowledgements

I would like to take this opportunity to thank all those who contributed their thoughts and ideas and allowed me permission to use photographs of their inspirational, creative settings and the invitations to learning their practitioners provide. It would not have been possible to get the breadth of examples without you, and I am so grateful to you all.

- Stone Hen Childcare
  - Laura Brothwell
- Nina's Nursery High Lane
  - Amanda Redwood and Charlotte Blackburn
- Lexis Heal
- Andreas Childcare
  - Andrea Booth
- Carly Wood
- Claire Wilson Childminder
- Cheeky Rascalz
  - Amanda Calloway
- Child First Moulton
  - Angela Green
- Jaci Pastrana
- Busy Bunnies Childminding
  - Imogen Eyre

- Butterflies of Britain (The Nature Play Centre)
  - Lindsay Moore
- Carlene Cox-Newton
- Dolce Daycare & Pre-School
  - Sheila Lucas – Atelierista
- Bright Stars Nursery
- Little Learners Corby
- Little Wise Owls Childminding
  - Hayley Dyke
- Little Mini Lighthouse Family Day Care
  - Dominique Adema
- Martine Crowley – Childminder
- Pre-School @ St Helens
  - Sophie Strudwick
- Scallywags Nursery Chelmsford
  - Abbie-May Moore
- The Forest Approach
  - Wendy Hamley
- Aylesbury Vale Academy Pre-School
  - Zoe Clark
- Reflections Nursery & Small School
  - Martin Pace
- Neston Farm Nursery
- Reggio & Co
  - Candice Schoolman
- Love of Learning Childcare LLC
  - Ashley Corcoran

Thanks also to the amazing parents at Wally's Day Nursery for the opportunity to work every day with your inquisitive, curious toddlers and pre-school children. There was so much joy in working towards the images in this book and putting together content for the invitations that have featured. Of course, it goes without saying I am eternally grateful to the children who made it all possible and continue to surprise me every day with their growing personalities and talents.

To the staff who care for them, Tracey, Katy, Rosanna, Dawn, Sue, Lucy and Elaine, our children are lucky to have you with them every single day, sharing both the joy and challenges that are associated with this age group. You brought enjoyment, inspiration and, above all else, creativity to everything we did. And to Jessica, for always being behind the lens when I need you, capturing the moments that matter.

Special Thanks

To my own children, Theiah and Myllo, for continuing to provide inspiration as you grow into strong, confident children, forever providing adventures and smiles. My parents, Elaine and Keith, and my in-laws, Julie and Jim, I will be forever grateful for your support, words of reassurance and, of course, weekend sleepovers.

Most of all, to my husband, Martin, the one who is always there with love, endless cups of tea and a word of encouragement when it's needed. I couldn't have done it without you.

Contact: discover.creativity@outlook.com

Introduction

When I first embarked upon my journey into writing about young children and creativity, there were lots of things I wanted to share: my passion for early years and the creation of environments for young children to thrive in being some of them, as well as the knowledge I have gained following almost eighteen years in the profession, giving those in the sector or those looking to join it an interesting read and, hopefully, a starting point for their journey into what creative practice might look like. What I didn't foresee was all the things I'd learn along the way, and writing itself became a journey of knowledge and research of looking deeper into why we do what we do every day. The early education of young children has always been a passion of mine, and as such, it was always inevitable that I would build a career ensuring that they receive the highest-quality care and early learning within our family-run day nursery. It is also this passion that drives my desire to help others reflect on the quality of experiences they offer their children and families and improve their provision where necessary to make sure that the children's interests, fascinations and needs are at the forefront of practice.

My first book, *Discover Creativity with Babies*, focussed on developing creativity with very young children in early years settings up to the age of 2 years old. It featured a variety of examples from different types of provision and provided inspiration for those working with babies in early years settings and home-based settings. The highlight of my career so far was seeing it in print and knowing it was now available to those who wanted guidance and support in their role. It provided ideas for ways they could reflect on their practice and ensure that they were supporting the youngest children in thoughtful, stimulating environments based on the needs of the children they care for, not just what they may have seen on social media. Having written about the beauty of creativity with babies, the next step was to follow with a book designed for those working with children aged 2 and over in early years settings. Following a similar trajectory to the first, this book will look in more detail at the concept of creativity and how we can support its development with those children who are in toddler rooms and pre-schools around the country.

This book can be seen as a direct response to the suggestion that there is very little research or literature surrounding children under the age of 3 in early childhood settings. This can make

DOI: 10.4324/9781003271710-1

it difficult for those working with young children to find the information and inspiration they need based on such young children, and they are often left searching social media for picture-perfect settings that they can recreate without the true understanding of why. This book, alongside *Discover Creativity with Babies*, can be used by all those working with young children up to the age of 5 to gain further understanding of the underpinning theory of our sector and the ever-changing curriculums within it, as well as provides case studies and images from a range of real settings that give details of their rationale for creating the environments they have and the invitations they provide for young children.

Context

We have seen, particularly throughout the last few years, a shift in the way early years and the unwavering dedication of the sector have been viewed. Early years has seen a lot of change, from having to get to grips with the new inspection framework, only to months later be thrown into a challenging new normal as many fought their way through the coronavirus pandemic in 2020. The country faced a national lockdown and settings were closed to all but vulnerable children and those with parents whose jobs were seen as paramount to the COVID-19 response, and yet many early years settings and their staff worked tirelessly throughout. For many, it was not financially viable to open to so few children, so they closed their doors, for some, never to open again. Others have remained, on the edge but fighting to survive in what was an already underappreciated, underfunded and undervalued role. Yes, a new appreciation dawned, but here we are, still being underfunded and now fighting a new battle. Settings nationally are seeing a rise in children with speech and language delays, a lack of physical skills and resilience, and with low self-esteem and social abilities. Through no fault of their own, children have lacked the social interaction and communicative role models that are vital in the first three years of life. Whole cohorts of toddlers and pre-school children who have never known a life without masks and hand sanitiser are now struggling to read body language and gestures, lacking communication and language skills that should be rapidly developing at this age, but instead, we are seeing a rise in speech and language referrals and special educational needs advice.

In the UK, the early years foundation stage (EYFS), which consists of statutory requirements and non-statutory guidance, makes up the curriculum for settings and schools caring for children under the age of 5. Jones writes, 'here is the idea that adults shape and form children. They channel, direct and govern the way their children develop' (2009:25). Sadly, this indicates that despite recent changing attitudes as to what children are capable of and a revision of the EYFS, it seems as long as there are such systems in place that effectively govern what adults can and cannot do with the children they work with, adults can never really be free to explore with the child at their own pace and share in what the child thinks and feels. As stated in the statutory guidance, the early years foundation stage 'promotes teaching and learning to ensure children's "school readiness"' (DfE, 2014:7). Egan goes some way to disagree with this as a reason for imposing a curriculum on the under 5s and suggests that it should 'never be merely instrumental to achieving other goals' (Pound, 2011:123), something which the current framework appears to be, as it seems that the focus is on preparing for school and not, as it perhaps should be, on the child. In support of the current framework for early years in the UK, the emotional development of a child is seen as vital for encouraging creativity. Numeracy and literacy, however, act as 'elements that conspire against creativity' (Sharp, 2004:8). This provides a reason why literacy and mathematics are placed within the specific areas of learning as opposed to the prime areas.

It is important that practitioners feel listened to and that the context in which children are living is reflected. There is a growing body of literature that is beginning to focus on younger children and their early years experiences, but it is still the case that those under 3 and practitioners who care for them remain largely underrepresented. This is reiterated by Graue and Walsh (1998), who argue that despite the numerous research projects that exist, there is still very little known about their lives and 'the contexts in which children live' (1998:1).

We must acknowledge children's feelings, too, and ensure we understand that their emotions often come from a place of need. As children over the age of 2 are the primary focus of this book, it stands to reason that we try to understand their unique needs and grow with them at this exciting time of development. For some reason, when children turn 2, they are expected to behave in a completely different way than those under 2. As babies, we expect them to cry as a form of communication, and we often go to them, ready to interpret and meet their needs. Why then, as soon as they turn 2, do we expect them to behave differently? We expect them to listen, sit still for a story and behave, all of which are developmentally inappropriate. Children need uninterrupted time to play, to express themselves and to do this within the boundaries that are set for them by adults. If they do not have these opportunities, children become unable to play without support, become unable to make decisions and rely on adult acceptance and reassurance before carrying out tasks. All of which are not conducive to the development of creativity. Play is active learning, and children do not need to be formally taught in their earliest years; however, there is still a tendency in this country to focus on what children of pre-school age are learning. The free entitlement funding for 3- and 4-year-olds of fifteen hours per week and the extended entitlement of thirty hours funded by the government are the most likely reasons for this. Unfortunately, it has always been the case that wherever money is being spent, those who are spending it want to know where it is going and what it is being spent on. For those in government, this means imposing rules on how providers can use the entitlement to support children and being clear that it must cover the education of children. For this reason, those in pre-schools are often subject to audits, repaying funding (for example, if a child leaves the provision) regardless if it had already been spent on improving quality and stringent guidelines from their local education authorities, all whilst trying to provide the best care and education for young children and continuing to try and make ends meet, as the funding rate often doesn't even cover the hourly rate charged by providers.

Chapter summary

For the purpose of this book, I have defined toddlers as those children aged between 2 and 3 years old, although recognise that for some settings (including my own), they may have slightly younger children grouped accordingly. For instances where I focus on pre-school-age children, I will be referring to those aged 3 and above, although again, realise that settings may have children between the ages of 2 and 5 in their pre-school spaces, and others may break these age groups into smaller rooms. Each chapter in this book represents an important part of our understanding about young children from the age of 2 in our early years settings and how we can acknowledge the importance of creativity whilst promoting it within our practice.

Chapter 1 outlines key elements of creativity and some of the historical definitions that shape the way we think about its development in children from the age of 2. It will explore the development of children's divergent thinking as well as how we can foster curiosity and imagination to ensure that children develop many of the skills vital for creative thinking.

In Chapter 2, we will specifically look at 2- and 3-year-olds, typically referred to as toddlers in early years settings. At this stage in their development, their brains are growing rapidly, and they are attempting to make sense of the world through their interactions with others and the opportunities we provide for them. Creativity is about taking risks and making connections, something that, by their nature, toddlers are very good at. It stands to reason then that they need an environment that allows this to occur as well as practitioners who understand how important it is that children are allowed to make their own decisions. I will discuss how adults can use transitional times to support young children's independence and how the behaviour and expectations displayed by toddlers can be respectfully observed and managed to ensure they continue to develop a strong sense of self. Chapter 3 follows a similar course with children from the age of 3 and typically attending pre-schools. This also includes those who will, following their fourth birthday, start their formal education in primary school. For these children, it is even more important that they get as much time to play as possible because despite still falling into the category of early years, reception classes all too often expect children to sit for long periods, reducing the time they have for play. 'These academic activities are time consuming for both child and teacher; and what little time is allocated to play is termed structured play – the intention being to serve numeracy or literacy goals or some other adult-imposed intention' (Oldfield, 2001:49).

The underpinning theory behind our practice will be explored in Chapter 4, using the pioneers of early years, such as Susan Isaacs, John Dewey and Loris Malaguzzi. It is not often that we consider where our ideas come from. For the most part, our education, experiences and social interactions are responsible for the way we think and the way we choose to do things. In practice, much of what we do is inspired by others, but it is important to consider our own why. Using social media and living in a technologically advanced world have their advantages, and simply sharing practice and knowledge with likeminded professionals has become much easier; however, there must be a warning attached that unless it reflects the lives of the children we are working with and the needs of those children, it will produce very little of the same impact, if any at all. In this chapter, we will also look at several examples of how settings have embedded the early thinkers into their practice and approach to the curriculum. Chapter 5 will take an in-depth look at the relationships that are formed with children in the years following their second birthday and how practitioners can ensure they are respectful and acknowledge the growing personality and needs of the child. We revisit boundaries and expectations of children who are beginning to challenge authority and how we can support them through some periods where we often see big emotions. Children need quality interactions at a time when their understanding of a social world is developing; this is something we will also explore within this chapter as well as detail some of the ways practitioners can tailor their interactions to young children, ensuring that they are building on their knowledge and extending their play to support creativity.

Chapter 6 focusses on the environment that is required to foster and encourage creativity. We will explore some of the ways practitioners can reflect on what they offer and ensure it continually meets the needs of the children. This chapter breaks down elements of the environment and discusses them in detail, including the emotional and physical space we afford older children and how lighting, colour and the organisation of the environment all have a vital role to play. The resources we have for children and how we present them is important when we consider how creativity manifests itself. This is the focus of Chapter 7. We know, with their growing sense of autonomy, children often want to do things for themselves, so what we provide and ensuring it is accessible is vital. We will look at what constitutes quality resources when working with young children and how to ensure we remain as environmentally and budget-friendly as possible at a time when settings are trying to be extremely conscious of this.

There has been a huge increase in the number of children who have limited access to the outdoors in recent years, and this is having a negative effect on a range of skills that we associate with young children. Children lack core strength, the ability to sit still and have poor posture, among many other signs that all is not well with their physical development. As Angela Hanscom explains, 'children are getting weaker, less resilient and less imaginative. They're having trouble paying attention in school, experiencing difficulty controlling emotions and having trouble safely navigating their environment' (2016:30). In the last chapter of Part 1, we will look in more depth at the outdoors and how children can be supported within nature to develop holistically. Whilst we know that there are many benefits to being in nature and engaging in outdoor play to improve all areas of learning, too many children are still not getting enough time to play uninterrupted outdoors. This chapter will also look at ways we can change this through practitioners' and leaders' reflective practice.

Within the context of the early years foundation stage in the UK, Chapter 9 looks at how creative play can be used by practitioners to cover many aspects of learning and development, and ensure the children in their care are receiving meaningful experiences. I will briefly explore process art and what we mean when we talk about *activities*, *invitations* and *provocations*, as understanding these terms is crucial to providing high-quality experiences. In Chapters 10 through 13, I present a range of engaging and easy-to-prepare invitations to create and play for children from the age of 2, ensuring that practitioners are mindful in their interactions and respect the child's emerging autonomy. As personal, social and emotional development can be embedded within all opportunities, this will be reflected throughout the subsequent chapters. Chapter 10 focusses primarily on developing ways of cooking with young children, whilst Chapter 11 includes ways to support language and communication. Most of the invitations to play or create require minimum setup time (essential when working with young children), and practitioners should encourage the children to help get it ready and clean up when it has been finished; giving children responsibility is a great way to develop their self-esteem. Most, if not all, can also be achieved on a budget. Most settings are becoming increasingly aware of funding and budget constraints, and so it is my intention to provide cost-effective, easy and achievable ideas that will support the developing creative mind, giving children the freedom to express themselves alongside present, observing practitioners. Chapter 12 looks at physical activities, supporting fine and gross motor skills, and finally, in Chapter 13, we look at the outdoors and how best to utilise the space you have to get the most from your environment.

Final note

The purpose of this book was always to be as accessible as possible for those working with children from the age of 2, regardless of the type of provision you have. I have been lucky enough to have contributions from a range of practitioners, including those working from their homes, those working in smaller settings and those who have larger provision with over fifty children every day. 'Early years staff can help young children to develop their creativity by providing a creative environment, helping children to build up their skills through play, behaving creatively themselves and praising children's creative efforts' (Sharp, 2004:9), and my hope is that the breadth of examples, combined with the knowledge I have shared, provides inspiration to practitioners, leaders and managers on how this is possible and that they are able to consider their own practice and environments through the use of reflection activities in order to provide the best quality of creative experiences and opportunities for the children they work with, ensuring that the children remain always at the heart of why they do what they do each day.

Part I

Looking deeper at creativity

In this chapter, we will look deeper into the notion of creativity and what it means for children in their early years. In the first book in this series, *Discover Creativity with Babies*, a definition of *creativity* was established by looking at several well-known writers and their models of creativity. The definition given by Pascal and Bertram (2017:1) states that 'creativity is imaginative activity fashioned as to produce something (process or outcome) which is both original and of value'. In this chapter, we will revisit this definition and the concept of creativity and explore some of the elements that aid our understanding, including imagination, problem-solving and agency, to establish how we can ensure we are providing ample opportunities for young children to develop and maintain their creativity in the years before formal schooling begins.

DOI: 10.4324/9781003271710-3

Definition

Many who have attempted to define *creativity* before me know;

> there are far too many different and interesting ideas about the nature of creativity to include in one book, much less one chapter and, as a result, many important ideas and worthwhile perspectives on creativity will be omitted in what follows.
>
> (Baer, 1993:5)

This is important to acknowledge because the nature of creativity and its many facets ensure that it is unlikely we will ever know the true meaning of what it is to be creative.

There are four definitions that have shaped the way we think about creativity, and whilst we have seen that many share similar ideas, each of these definitions places value on a different aspect. The definitions are as follows:

1   'Creativity is the generation of ideas that are both novel and valuable' (Boden, 1999:351). We can see here a focus on the person.

2   'A creative response to a problem is new, good and relevant' (Kaufman & Sternberg, 2007:55). The product is the focus in this definition.

3   'Mental processes that lead to solutions, ideas, conceptualisations, artistic forms, theories or products that are unique or novel' (Johnson-Laird, 1988:203).

4   'Imaginative activity fashioned as to produce outcomes that are both original and of value' (NACCCE, 1999:30). This, and the definition given by Johnson-Laird, focus on the product of creativity.

We can, of course, examine some of the most important elements of creativity, something which this chapter will explore; however, producing a definition that encompasses all the facets of creativity is almost impossible and perhaps should remain as such. What I mean by this is if we truly understood the nature of creativity and how to produce more of it in our young children and adults (if indeed we were able), the very worrying possibility that we would lose what it means to be creative would become a reality. It is true that there have been hundreds of definitions of creativity over the years; each one comes with its own ideas about what it involves and if we can nurture it into being. The reason for this is most likely because when we talk about creativity, there are so many interpretations of exactly what we mean. Anna Craft (2002) suggests that the nearest definitions to the truth are those that involve several elements. Mohammed (2018) also suggests that there are common threads that run through all the definitions.

Creative thinking

Creativity is an important part of intelligence, but the scientific community has struggled to clearly define it. If we step back for a moment and consider whether we believe ourselves to be creative individuals, we have some insight into how ownership of creativity works. No doubt we have heard practitioners say that they are not creative or that other colleagues are the creative ones. It might even be you who thinks you are not creative, leaving tasks requiring a creative mind to others. At what point do we stop believing creativity is something we possess and is a trait of others? It could be that practitioners who think in this way believe they are no good at drawing, painting or coming up with ideas, but creativity is so much more than that, and if we don't believe it about ourselves, how can we begin to encourage the skills children need to develop it effectively?

Creative thinking is the process we use to develop ideas that are original and useful; this fits with the definition given by Pascal and Bertram (2017). It is the ability to think of original and diverse ideas, and to elaborate on those ideas. It includes the process of using divergent thinking and thinking of multiple options, but it is also playing with those ideas internally and through the possibilities and resources we have available to us. Thinking in possibilities, being flexible and thinking of new combinations using our ideas are things we now know are crucial to creative thinking. Creative thinking encompasses open-mindedness, flexibility and adaptability, and is something that we should all be striving to support in our settings. To develop creative thinking, children need 'opportunities to explore ideas and materials and to make choices about activities' (Fumoto et al., 2012:32).

Play

Play, as we will see throughout this book, is the cornerstone of all future development. We know that children who do not have enough time to play, unrestricted by adults, show much lower levels of creative skills, such as problem-solving and imagination, than their peers who have had the opportunity to engage in prolonged periods of play. Craft, even in 2002, noted 'the accelerating spiral of change in technology is another element which both responds to, and feeds change' (2002:43). This is even more relevant now and is the reason so many children are missing vital opportunities to play with their peers. Lives are becoming busier; parents are finding it more and more difficult to make ends meet with rising costs of living, and many are taking several jobs at a time. This means that children are being left with grandparents or friends, as the cost of childcare is also increasing. Children seem to be spending prolonged amounts of time in front of screens, and more importantly, all this is happening alongside restricted access to the outdoors, too. It is easy to see why the decline in free play is so prevalent in this country, and with technology advancing at an alarming rate, it doesn't look set to improve.

This means that managers and practitioners have an important role in ensuring that our children have as much time to play as possible. Play and playfulness are important for our understanding of creativity and can help explain why 'children tend to be seen as a pure embodiment of creativity' (Glaveanu, 2021:16). This is echoed by Sharp (2004), who asserts that children are highly creative and possess a natural tendency to explore and experiment within their environment; therefore, we must provide opportunities for children 'to try out and play with ideas, to speculate and hypothesize and to use their imaginations, both alone and with others' (Fumoto et al., 2012:32).

REFLECTION

Consider, as a team, how much of the children's day is dictated by adults.

Too often, we believe that children are having long, uninterrupted periods to play, but is that really the case?

In between snack time, lunchtime, quiet time and other activities, how many hours are the children actually busy playing?

Write down the routine of your day (as far as you can); now look at how small changes can improve the amount of time children can play uninterrupted.

Curiosity

When we consider some of the characteristics that make up a creative mind, curiosity usually comes first. Without it, children would be unable and perhaps even unwilling to explore their surroundings and what their bodies can do. Children are naturally curious from birth. They gaze at faces and copy movements and facial expressions as they try and find out about themselves within a social context. As children get older, this curiosity needs to be nurtured. Children need to develop an awareness of their surroundings, and the only way to do this is to explore freely with a sense of curiosity, awe and wonder.

Whilst we know that children are innately interested in the world, what becomes clear as they get older is the notion that, as practitioners, we must facilitate this curiosity by first understanding how important it is to the child and their overall development. Curiosity underpins much of what life is like in the first five years; however, we also know that children who do not have access to a rich learning environment and mindful, trusting practitioners find it difficult to engage in open-ended play and dialogue with others. For pre-school children, the most effective way to promote curiosity is by posing questions and encouraging young children to think about different ways to do things. However, what is equally as important is how we respond to those questions.

If we want children to explore their world and think critically, it is of no benefit to provide the answers to their questions without first pausing for thought. If we answer everything they ask, their desire to continue their investigation diminishes. Instead, consider asking another question, such as 'how do you think we could find out?', encouraging them to develop the skills they need to answer their own questions and continue in their discoveries.

'If a child asks, "how many legs does a spider have?" instead of offering the correct answer outright, encourage the child to find the answer' (Johnson & Watts, 2019:23). By doing so, children can test their ideas, think about ways of doing things and develop further their ability to think creatively.

Imagination

'This involves thinking and involves bringing about something that did not exist or was not known before, so it had to be imagined first. This can imply that the imagination first needs to be stimulated to lead to creativity' (Mohammed, 2018:2). If this is the case, then children must be exposed to opportunities where they can express themselves and their ideas freely with a range of resources. From the age of 2, we can begin to see the way children use their imaginations in play. Practitioners often observe young children applying the characteristics of a telephone to a banana or a brick, walking around with it held at their ear. Many are old enough to know that it is not in fact a telephone, but it is their imaginative skill that allows them to begin to pretend. This is something that is vital to future development. The ability to think innovatively when we do not have the resources we need will certainly come in handy. At Wally's Day Nursery, children's narratives are respected, and children move freely around the environment, collecting what they need to continue their storytelling.

As children begin to develop their understanding further, role-play activities initiated by the children become more collaborative as they engage in the same theme; for example, a game of families. Children take what they know about the world and often imitate it. If a child has a new sibling at home, they are likely to model caring for the dollies. If they recently took a family pet to the vets, they may add a narrative into their play that reflects this, all the time building on what they know already and extending it alongside their peers. Children at Nina's Nursery Highlane engage in imaginative play daily, alongside authentic resources and different media.

Interaction here is important as we extend what children already know and encourage them to think critically. Helicopter stories are a fantastic way not only to promote self-confidence and esteem in young children but to develop their literacy, language and imaginative skills. The beauty of helicopter stories is that it is quick to implement, meaning the impact, if done properly, will be seen sooner. Children are invited to act out stories read by a narrator (usually a practitioner), and when they feel able, they progress to telling their story so the practitioner can scribe, choosing a character and having an audience. There is great curiosity in listening to a child and wondering where their ideas come from. It is this that is 'the most exciting aspect of the work. We are engaged on a journey. It is improvisation and neither I nor the children know where the stories will take us' (Lee, 2016:5). By 'encouraging children to use their imagination, adults are supporting children to use their creative thinking skills' (Johnson & Watts, 2019:24).

Agency

We are beginning to see that creativity requires 'freedom and control; the freedom to experiment and the control of skills, knowledge and understandings' (DfES, 1999:38). The problem with this is that many practitioners are still not at the point where they are ready to give the children in their care the agency required to fully embrace this. Instead, they are concerned that 'when children are being creative, they are more likely to be troublesome and disobedient' (May, 2009:14). This is having a detrimental effect on our young children, as staff are not able or remain unwilling to give them the freedom and opportunity to choose.

Having a strong sense of agency is important for young children as they develop their identity. When children have agency and the right environment, they can act independently of others appropriate for their age. They have the confidence to ask for help when they need it and can make choices about how they spend their time. These children engage and connect with those around them, explore their surroundings and, in this way, come to develop a strong sense of self. Children who are less confident, however, tend to act in response to the expectations of others and are likely not to begin activities on their own or to become involved in what they are doing. These children will not have experienced the opportunities to develop their sense of agency due to overly restrictive environments, perhaps too much authority or unnecessarily being reprimanded for exercising their agentic behaviour. It can be difficult to encourage children to engage when they have been unable to experience freedom of choice and self-expression, but it can be done. Through supportive practitioners and an environment that is accessible and encourages independence, expression and, most of all, values the child for their ideas, children will become more confident and eventually learn they can express themselves in a way they choose.

The key element of agency and freedom, it seems, is that children feel a sense of belonging within their environment and with the people who care for them. In order to embed this sense of value and approach children with the respect they deserve, practitioners must listen and engage with children at their pace on a level they understand.

REFLECTION

Find a space in the room where you work and sit down back to back with one of your colleagues. It helps if you can each see one side of the room.

Now take it in turns to describe one feature of your environment, and your colleague must respond with ways it can promote children's agency. Do this until you have considered most aspects of your environment.

Come together to reflect on any area that you found difficult and look for ways you can encourage children's independent choices.

Listening to young children: the Mosaic approach

The Mosaic approach has three distinct stages that support practitioners in listening to young children, understanding them and acting on what they find out. The research that led to the development of the Mosaic approach, suggested that in order for children to feel valued and part of their respective communities, they needed to be listened to. Not in a tokenistic way, but truly listening to children, even those who are non-verbal, can ensure that we support them so they feel a sense of belonging and that they are valued and respected as human beings. If children feel valued, their sense of self and wellbeing greatly increases, and their ability to feel confident in making choices leads to deeper levels of engagement and creative thinking.

We have to acknowledge children's feelings, too, and ensure we understand that their emotions often come from a place of need.

So often children are punished for being human. They are not allowed to have grumpy moods, bad days, disrespectful tones or bad attitudes. Yet, we adults have them all the time . . . we must stop holding our children to a higher standard of perfection than we can attain ourselves.

(Rebecca Eanes)

Creativity in practice

Staff at Nina's Nursery High Lane place creativity and freedom of thought high on their agenda, resulting in environments and resources that foster creative thinking in young children.

We understand that not every member of staff has an artistic flair, some are creative and some not so much. Some staff don't think they are when actually they have an eye for creating beautiful invitations to play rather than being avid painters. This acknowledgement that everyone has an important skill to bring to the team empowers the staff to feel confident within their practice and also to share their skills amongst the team. Each evening the setting is thoughtfully set up with varied invitations and provocations to play, opportunities to be creative are weaved throughout these whether it's the main Art Area having plentiful resources for the children to investigate or the Home Corner and Construction area having extensions of mark making resources. The staff also do their own research on invitations they can create by looking at past activities, following other practitioners and settings or simply searching the internet for seasonal investigations. Within all of these opportunities the children are always focused at the centre, with activities being devised from their interests and extended by thoughtful interactions that leave the children still free to explore but supported if and when required.

By acknowledging staff as a resource, settings have more chance of engaging children in something that interests them. Staff can draw on their own lived experiences and incorporate these into their daily practices, environment and interactions with children, ensuring that they promote creativity in many different ways. This is just some of the examples of best practice that demonstrate how children can be supported to develop the skills they need for creativity. Throughout this book, I will provide examples from the many professionals I have had the pleasure of working with of how they have interpreted creativity and how they encourage it at their setting. Each one advocates for the best possible early years experience for their children where they are gifted time, freedom and choice, three vital elements in the development of creativity.

Conclusion

We assume that those individuals who study fine arts and other creative courses are more creative, but important research has been done on whether or not creativity was more prevalent based on their area of study. It found that art students are not inherently more creative; art education is designed to foster creative thinking skills through the use of a sensory anchor, being engaging and encouraging rich connections (Moga et al., 2000). It is clear from this research that it is the environment we create for young children that will have the greatest impact in their development of creative thinking and that if we don't make sure we are doing all we can, 'creativity can be impeded' (Craft, 2002:9). Creativity is vital to children's future life chances and opportunities and, therefore, should be embedded within early years practice and training courses designed for new practitioners to the sector, to ensure that they understand not only how it manifests itself in young children but also how to support and encourage it through the environments, interactions and resources we share with them.

In terms of a definition of creativity that resonates with the purpose of this book and the themes that we will explore, it is Pascal and Bertram (2017:1) that we return to.

> Creativity is imaginative activity fashioned as to produce something (process or outcome) which is both original and of value.

This is because it places importance on the 'processes that children engage with in their learning environment, which is not necessarily outcome-based: the outcome is the child's choice to make' (Mohammed, 2018:31). In their explanation, they feel 'this definition could be applied to a whole range of learning areas and affordances for learning, and that it embraces a wide range of cognitive, emotional and social/relational processes' (Pascal & Bertram cited in Mohammed, 2018:31).

In terms of the current curriculum in the early years, although it highlights that children's creativity must be extended by supporting their natural curiosity, exploration and play and children must be provided with opportunities to explore and share their thoughts, creativity, ideas and feelings, recent research has shown that lifelong creativity in children is a more intrinsic, holistic process than simply providing children the opportunity to learn through play. Practitioners need an understanding of this to embed a culture of creativity with the children they work with and ensure they provide as many rich, creative experiences as possible.

2 What it means to be a creative toddler

In this chapter, we will look into the idea of what it means to be a creative 2-year-old and how we can support children as they reach another important transition in their early years. In UK settings, this is usually the time practitioners start to think about moving children up to the next room, often with different expectations and opportunities for children to explore. For toddlers, it can be argued that everything they do has a creative undertone. What and how they choose to spend their time, what to play with at a given moment and how they use resources can all be seen through a creative lens if we just know how. Throughout this chapter, I will offer examples of what I believe it means to be a creative toddler, the practices in settings that support the model of creativity that allows children the freedom to express themselves and how children and the adults that care for them can work together to create a culture where creativity can thrive.

DOI: 10.4324/9781003271710-4

There are many types of childcare providers, from childminders and home day care to larger day nurseries and pre-schools, and each one will organise the children they care for differently. For those in smaller settings and those at home, the number of children and the age of those children can vary greatly, meaning their definition of a *toddler* may be different than perhaps that of a sessional pre-school who, if they take children from the age of 2 and half, may not refer to them as toddlers at all. This is perhaps the first problem settings face when looking at the provision they have for young children, as it can be difficult to ensure age-appropriate resources and environments when there is such a broad age range grouped together. In this chapter, we will consider toddlers as those between 2 and 3 years of age. A full year of varying behaviours, feelings and attitudes that are constantly changing as the children continue to find their place, experience the world and build relationships with those around them.

Brain development

When we think about toddlers, we envisage young children who walk, run, are full of innate curiosity, have a unique zest for life and, usually, but not always, are on the go most of the day. Although there are exceptions to this based on an individual's temperament or background and previous experiences, when we think of toddlers, rightly or wrongly, we associate a particular set of characteristics and behaviours.

The behavioural changes that can occur in the third year of life are intense for even the most seasoned practitioner, but it is important to respect these changes, allow children to feel their emotions rather than try and control them, and employ appropriate strategies and responses to ensure we are supporting children to effectively develop the skills they need to eventually manage the big emotions they feel when they are developmentally ready. The experiences children encounter in the first three years of their life have a huge impact on their future life chances and the skills they begin to learn in their toddler years will stay with them and develop throughout their childhood. One such skill is that of self-regulation, and we can start to see the importance of this skill as it has, for the first time, been included in the revised early years foundation stage, alongside managing self and building relationships. It is a complex concept often described as the way a person is able to recognise and manage their feelings and behaviours in a way that would be deemed acceptable to others. Someone with the ability to regulate their feelings effectively will exhibit other abilities too, such as solving problems, having appropriate interactions with others and controlling their behaviour.

It comes as no surprise then that young children, who are just starting out on their journey of self-regulation,

find it difficult to do these things. This is where the practitioners' work really starts; children are not born with the skills they need to self-regulate. They need the adults in their lives to support them and respond to them appropriately in the process of co-regulation, as this will help them to develop meaningful relationships and learn that they can rely on others to help them when they need it. As children develop their sense of autonomy, practitioners need to ensure they are still present so that the connections in the brain can continue to grow. Without clear boundaries, there is the potential for disruptive behaviour, tantrums and children in the throw of emotional turmoil. Practitioners have a unique role when working with toddlers to show them what boundaries can look like in the context of their settings whilst also educating parents as to what appropriate boundaries for 2-year-olds look like at home and how to ensure the two stay consistent.

Transition

For children in day nurseries, the change once you turn 2 can be huge; the transition from baby rooms with a 1:3 ratio (in the UK) to often larger spaces with a larger number of children can mean a period of adjustment for young children that isn't seen in home-based education settings. Many nurseries in the UK have specific ages in each of their rooms, meaning that regardless of the child's development and readiness to progress to the next stage in their learning, they are moved around the setting according to birthday. This can result in a prolonged period of settling into a new room for young children if not done according to the child's needs. Although this is a common practice (mainly due to the change in ratio when a child reaches 2 years old and then again when they turn 3, making staffing a lot easier to manage), it isn't necessarily what is best for the child and is why it is so important, if you do work this way, that any transition is done in a way to minimise anxiety not only for the child but for their parents, too.

At my setting, we use a developmental approach, whereby children are moved into the next room when they are ready and not when dictated to do so by their birthday. We respect fully the child's developmental path, and in doing so, children benefit from a much smoother transition process that they are ready for. We know that typically developing children will all follow the same developmental pathway, but the rate at which they do so can differ greatly; it is important, therefore, that they are given the time they need to develop the skills required to manage the transition to another room or setting.

From around the age of 20 months (if they are ready), our children begin the transition into the toddler room, but we also have scope to keep children beyond 2 in our baby room provision if moving rooms would cause distress or prove a challenge for them. Information is gathered from parents about the things their child enjoys and their current routine so that staff can support them through the transition either from room to room or on entry to the setting. Ratio must be adjusted if children under 2 join the toddler room, and understandably, this is only possible in some cases. I am fully aware that for those settings who rely on a certain number of staff in each of their rooms and don't have this flexibility, it can be more difficult to use this approach. It is even more important then that those settings who move children dependent on their birthday ensure that the environment and resources are set up in response to a child's individual developmental needs, as they may not be entirely ready for what is expected of them.

Routines and flexibility

One such expectation that is often seen in toddler rooms is the structure of a routine. Young children in baby rooms will have had little experience of sticking to a particular routine, other than perhaps that of feeding and sleeping. Once they make the transition into a toddler room, though, in most instances, that expectation changes, and very quickly, they are thrust into a structure that they are not familiar with, which can result in feelings of sadness, anger and frustration for young children.

Toddlers need flexibility and freedom to develop the necessary skills required for higher level thinking as they grow. Routines form an important part of our settings, whether that's a small home-based childminder or larger day nurseries; we couldn't function without them, but that doesn't mean they have to be rigid, military operations or conveyor belts of practical jobs to be done, especially where toddlers are concerned. For adults as well as children, it's important to know what is going on and what must be done throughout the day; we know that mealtimes are integral as well as perhaps toileting and hand-washing and perhaps, for some, group time involving songs or stories for the children. The way in which these activities are done can vary greatly, though, and this is where flexibility is crucial.

Some settings have set times for certain activities and may want to ensure all the children sit together at the same time for meals or snack times. There are some nurseries who have group time with their 2-year-olds, where they are encouraged to sit or stand together at a particular activity for a set amount of time, or others who encourage free play and no guided interventions for the majority of the day. What is important here, regardless of how the day is structured, is that the routines are relevant to the children in your setting and what their current developmental needs are. Doing something because you've always done it or because someone tells you to is not enough of a reason to keep doing it. Children need consistency, but this doesn't have to mean that every day is the same, and this certainly shouldn't be the case when working with 2-year-olds.

Part of the joy in working with toddlers is the unpredictability of them. What works one day may not work the next, and this will depend entirely on their mood, their interests and how they started their day. We know that toddlers are largely governed by their need to be in control, as is normal at this age, so trying to compartmentalise their day for them is always going to be difficult. It can lead to struggles between the child and practitioner, as the children are trying to assert their autonomy, and the adults who work with them are trying to enforce certain behaviours or actions. As those who work with young children know, these struggles can be draining, and for many practitioners, it results in them doing whatever it was they wanted the child to do in the first place themselves. Whilst not ideal, it is often easier than having to contend with several emotionally charged toddlers, something which many try to avoid. The simple response to this is to change or, at the very least, adapt the way we set routines and expectations to suit the needs of the children we work with. When routines are flexible, children are allowed the freedom to choose when and if to participate, something which is vital in the journey of discovery into the self and their emerging autonomy. Of course, I am not saying that routines should be so flexible that no one knows what they're doing one minute to the next, but a reflective conversation within your staff team will enable you to develop a way of doing things that meets the needs of both the children and the staff involved.

REFLECTION

■ Do you have set timings that are the same each day?

■ Do children have periods where they are disengaged because everyone has to do the same activity at the same time?

■ Do you have staff who are known as clock watchers within the team, making sure that everything is being done on time?

If you answered yes to any of these questions, it's time to reflect on why and what you can do to make small steps to change.

Tidying with toddlers

Toddlers love helping; they are at an age where their independence is growing rapidly, and they want to be involved. This is great news for us as practitioners, as it gives us a real opportunity to involve children in routines and rhythms of the day. They can begin to help with tidying up resources, setting up tables for lunch or snack and caring for plants or setting animals, all of which start them on their journey to learning about responsibility and their place in the setting. It is important to involve children as much as possible, as in doing so, it creates a culture of supporting and helping others, something which is fundamental to the future of a society. Too many times, practitioners flurry behind children, cleaning any mess they leave behind or waiting until the end of the day to tidy up the wreckage that is left. For those who hire commercial cleaners, great, they get left with the residue of the day, and no one has to take responsibility for the mess that has been created, least of all the children. For those who don't have an external company to come in and clean for them, they are often left working longer hours and staying later to tidy and then clean their rooms, ready for the next day when the cycle inevitably continues. If either of these scenarios resonate with you, perhaps it is time for reflection. Is there a better way to spend your day, free from cleaning up after children and more time to enjoy their play alongside them? No one said it would be easy, but it is doable with a little determination.

Toddlers can be encouraged to put things back where they belong with practitioners or to reset play spaces ready for the next day, and doing this throughout the day will reduce the time it takes when all the children have gone home. It doesn't have to be a tambourine-banging event that stops children from their deep levels of engagement or a special song that is sang by less than enthusiastic staff members. Children thrive on knowing what is expected of them (something we will cover later in the book), and ensuring that you maintain age-appropriate expectations of children will ensure they develop a sense of belonging and value within your setting. Placing value on resources and empowering children to do the right thing takes time, and you will need to reflect on your own practice to reframe the way you do things. Children already think creatively; when they hear tidy-up time, it's usually because something is coming – whether that is a mealtime or even time to go home – what follows is a rush of children throwing things in boxes and using their creativity to come up with hiding places for things if they don't know where they belong, just so they can be finished and move on. More often than not, this results in practitioners finding pieces of puzzles or looking for items long after the children have gone home just to put them in the right place. How much easier would it be if we supported the children to do this in the first place? To encourage them to put things back where they belong when they have finished with them, giving ownership of the environment to the children and allowing them the chance to show you that they can take responsibility for the resources that they use. Children as young as 2 can help put things away, and whilst they might not know where everything goes straight away, with supportive practitioners, they can learn and will eventually help those younger than themselves.

REFLECTION

- Do you use an object or song to signify tidy-up time in your setting?

If so, why? Reflect with your team the purpose of this and what message it sends to the children?

Consider:

Talk to the children about what they are doing, comment and use suggestions that indicate what you'd like the child to do but give them a chance to express their autonomy.

- Shall we put the bricks away then you can go outside?

- We don't want to lose the pieces, do we? Let's put them back.

Note

There is always (and more than likely) the possibility that a child will say no. That's okay, too. We want them to share their thoughts, share their opinions and begin to exert their sense of self; however, what is important is that you ensure you follow through with your words/actions. Children need guidance and support, and if they don't want to put things away, you can either turn it into a game (I'll do one brick, you do one brick) by taking turns or, in the case of a model or structure, allow them to leave it for a certain number of days with the opportunity to return to it. What is important is that whatever you have asked them to do, they must do themselves or with support. Tidying up for them because it is easier will only lead to further power struggles between the child and practitioner in the long run.

Creating a yes space

Something which is important when working with toddlers is having the knowledge and ability to create a yes space for children, something which can be a physical play space but also an emotional one, founded on mutual respect and knowledge of what children need at this age. A place where they have access to a wide range of age-appropriate resources and equipment and are free to choose how to use it without adult intervention.

This is something that practitioners can find quite difficult, and it isn't something that is taught on early years courses, so newly qualified practitioners often have only the setting they work in as a guide for what this looks like (if it exists at all). There are two ways that a yes space can be created, and both are important in developing a child's sense of self and ownership over their own ideas and thoughts. All spaces for children should be created with the yes concept in mind. A place where they are unlikely to be told no, an environment where children cannot get hurt and are free to use and play with whatever they find. In theory, this sounds easy. Of course, most, if not all, settings are vigilant in their risk assessment that children should rarely get hurt, and the nature of toddlers suggest that they can play where and with whatever they want during their day, but this isn't always the case.

There are settings where children are stopped from exploring, not allowed to climb to a particular height or to get mess on the carpet. There are practitioners who don't like mess (or having to clean it), who are scared children will get hurt if they take risks or who find it easier to have the children stationed at an activity, but why? Because it is easier for them. Children are perceived as easier to manage if they are kept together, herded from place to place and do things that are safe. We know from years of research into what has been called risky or adventure play that children need to challenge themselves in order to learn their own limits. They need opportunities to test their theories and see what their bodies are capable of alongside adults they can trust, and there is no better time to do this than with toddlers, who have very little fear and are ready and waiting to explore what they can do. This makes some practitioners uneasy, but it is my hope that you will begin reflecting on the feelings that cause you to think this way and think about the impact it is having on the children you work with.

Children are not made to stand still, wait their turn (unless developmentally appropriate) or listen to everything you say. It's part of their nature to challenge the boundaries and expectations we have of them, and by creating a yes space and thinking about the way we communicate with children, we can allow them the freedom to express their ideas, fascinations and interests.

In terms of the language we use with children, creating a yes space involves reframing what we say to allow children the opportunity to think for themselves. Instead of repeatedly telling a child, 'No, don't do that' or 'stop it, I said no', why not try and give children a yes space, a space where you don't have to tell them no. Of course, I'm not saying that you should remove boundaries. We know children need them. However, it's important that you respect the children and their wishes, and by providing a space where you don't always have to tell them no, children can begin to make their own decisions, and at 2, this is exactly what they need as they develop their autonomy and their view of themselves as strong and capable.

An example that demonstrates this point is those settings where practitioners have particular expectations of children regarding sand. In my setting, we have large immersive sandpits for the children to use in each of our rooms that cater for 2–5-year-olds, and how they choose to use these is completely open to interpretation by the children. Some settings, however, stipulate that in order to play in their sandpit, the children must take their shoes and socks off, the sand must not be moved or spilled over the edge of the tray or table, or the sand is only for indoors/outdoors. Here, we can begin to see where children's creativity and autonomy is being stifled by adult expectations at such a young age.

It is important to ask yourself why. Why do children need to keep the sand in one place? Why do they need to take their shoes and socks off? Often, it is for the benefit of the adult, not the child in these situations. We want it in one place so it's easier to clean, and we want their shoes and socks off so they won't spread sand around the carpet. If we step back and look at the lost opportunities and the messages we send children, we are telling them we are in control and we want things done our way. A child who goes into the sand with their shoes on may be encouraged to take them off, but what if they don't want to? What if they like to play in the sand but don't want it in their toes? There are two possible outcomes here, and neither will be as magical as the child's original. The first is that the child leaves the sand to remove their shoes and socks and then returns, but their thoughts and ideas may have been lost in the time it took to put their shoes on a shelf or in a basket. The second and worse still is that the moment is lost completely. The child may leave the sand area and, as they choose not to remove their shoes, are told they can't go in the sand. It is important to always reflect on the way you do things not to always keep rules and expectations because they've always been there. If a child wants to keep their shoes on in the sand, instead of going straight in asking them to remove them, why not observe the child and look at what they do in the sand and the way they manipulate it. This will ensure the child feels confident and, most importantly, respected; and when engaged, perhaps offer comments, such as, 'shall we see what it feels like on our toes?', therefore encouraging the child to take their shoes off, but instead of it being a condition of play, it is the child's choice by returning to that notion of agency and giving children the right conditions in which to exercise their options.

It is important to note that not all opportunities can be created in a yes space, so we must reflect also on our limitations. By acknowledging what we may find difficult to provide on a day-to-day basis, we are in a better position to offer alternatives. If you observe children climbing on chairs or over tables, try creating an obstacle course if space allows or taking them outside to climb trees and use language based on what you want the child to do whilst acknowledging their actions; for example, 'It looks like you want to climb but these tables are where we eat, why don't we go outside and see where/what we can climb'. By observing behaviour and providing alternatives, you are telling the children that you respect and trust them, and they will in turn feel listened to. It also allows children to fully explore their schematic interests without always feeling like they must conform.

REFLECTION

- Do you use provocations and invitations to play, excite and fascinate children, allowing them to choose what and how to participate?

- Ask instead of tell:

  - Would you like to . . . ?

  - Shall we . . . ?

  - I wonder, what happens if . . . ?

Think about how you frame your language so that children feel empowered to cooperate rather than coerced.

- Have resources that children can use to excess if they need to without staff trying to stop their play and explorations.

Boundaries and consequences

Boundaries and setting expectations for young children go hand in hand with agency, something that we will discuss in more detail in a later chapter. It is important that a setting has a clear strategy that everyone is aware of for dealing with boundaries, expectations and behaviour challenges but at the same time recognises that children are all different, with maturity levels, development and experiences from home that will all have an impact on the way they respond to directions or the needs of those around them. It is vital that we work in partnership with parents and identify from the beginning the ways in which parents prefer to set boundaries and the behaviour expectations at home. It can be very difficult trying to enforce expectations if they are different from what is expected in their home environment. For the most part, though, this is made easier, as parents choosing early years provision for their children will often choose settings based on their own values and expectations. The relationships we build with parents are crucial, as some children can spend up to (sometimes more than) fifty hours per week in childcare, so it is important that we mirror the expectations of home and ensure those children who are spending a prolonged period of time with us feel safe and trusted, and that we set boundaries allowing them to learn the nature of consequences whilst also developing their autonomy.

Working with 2-year-olds has its challenges, particularly if you work with a large group of them. They can be, by nature, egocentric and very often see things only from their perspective. Most are unable to communicate effectively enough to get their needs met independently, and some, particularly younger 2-year-olds, can still rely on adults to interpret their needs. This is why the language we use with young children is so important to get right. Even though they may still be reliant on adults for some things, as they develop, they will want more independence and will begin to push back against parents and adults who are trying to set boundaries and behavioural expectations. Two-year-olds can get easily frustrated, especially when things are not going their way or when they are trying to assert their authority. Those settings who have children between the ages of 2 and 5 in the same space have the difficult task of differentiating the needs and expectations of two very different stages in development, from the impulsive, exploratory just-2-year-old to the almost-5-year-old

primary school leaver. This is why it is vital that we take into account the child's level of development and maturity, and not apply a blanket behaviour policy, as what works for one child will not always work for them all. It is impossible to try and develop a strategy that applies to all children. In my experience, this isn't something that works well, and the reason for this is simple; all children are different.

Many of behaviours that are exhibited by children are a direct response to the world around them. It can be difficult to see past the child and their behaviour and look to your practices and setting, but that is the first thing that each of us, as professionals, need to do.

(Carlene Cox-Newton)

There are a range of different techniques that are used in trying to manage children's behaviour, from using sticker charts, timeouts, the high scope approach to conflict resolution as well as others that focus on the act of providing empathy, space and explanations to children. We will look at some of these in more detail in later chapters, but what should be acknowledged is that it should always be the child and their needs and feelings that are kept at the forefront of any strategy that is in place. It is not within the remit of this book to argue for a particular approach, behavioural strategy or way to deal with the challenges that may arise working with toddlers;

however, it is imperative that staff reflect on their own values, the ethos of their setting and what they believe children need and are capable of before prescribing to a particular approach and ensuring they have a firm understanding of why they are doing something, rather than keeping certain practices in place because that is how it has always been.

Engaging children in creative thinking

For children to engage with their environment and the people around them, and for them to begin to think in a way that could be considered creative, they must feel connected and have a sense of belonging. The spaces for children should be designed with them in mind, with opportunities for freedom and exploration at the heart of it. Typically, toddlers are at the age where they want to do everything for themselves, push boundaries and expectations, and are largely egocentric. The adults who care for them, therefore, have a responsibility to ensure that they have ample opportunities to make their own choices as this agentic behaviour develops. Of course, at 2 years old, we also have the very real responsibility of keeping them safe and ensuring that in making their own choices, they do not come to any harm, but with careful supervision and meaningful interaction, that is rarely the case.

There are many ways that we can support children by allowing them the time and space that they need to delve into their fascinations and schematic interests. Creativity is something that can be encouraged, using open-ended and authentic resources and observing and listening to children in their play. We know also that there are fundamental elements of creative play which include curiosity, imagination, opportunity to use problem-solving skills and the ability think openly and explore freely, and when all these elements are combined and supported with mindful practitioners, children's creative thinking can fully be engaged. When working with 2-year-olds, if we observe effectively, we will begin to see the underlying play interests of the children, and more often than not, it can tell us about their true interests. This is where observing and taking the time to notice what young children are doing are vital, as it can guide and inform what we provide in order to support their continuing creative thinking.

REFLECTION

As a team, have a look at the following schemas – can you identify children that you work with who display some of these behaviours and think about how can you support them?

- Enveloping: covering themselves or objects, wrapping toys in paper, covering dolls in blankets and playing peek-a-boo with scarves

- Enclosure: creating a barrier, enclosing oneself, creating barriers around objects, drawing circles or building fences

- Connection: putting objects together, taping things together, connecting blocks, building train tracks or building things and knocking them down

- Rotation: spinning in circles, rolling down hills (I still do this as an adult!), riding a bike in circles, pushing cars in circles or spinning a swing

- Trajectory: throwing or dropping things, or climbing and jumping off things

- Positioning: lining up toys or putting things in order

- Transporting: moving things from one area to another or filling baskets and bags, and transporting them around the room

- Transforming: mixing different materials together, or adding sand to paint or water to clay

To think creatively, children must be allowed to explore and investigate materials freely. Think about your environment. Is this something that you facilitate or are you forever telling children to put the sand back in the sand tray or keep all the loose parts together?

Reflect as a team and think about ways you can create a yes space for children to explore freely their schematic interests.

Chapter summary

Throughout this chapter, we have explored some of the key elements that feature heavily in the lives of 2-year-olds in early years settings. We have touched on the importance of understanding children's development at a time when there are thousands of new connections being made in the brain as children find their own way in early years settings and learn how to use strategies to cope with starting at a new setting. We know that young children need supportive adults, something we will cover in a later chapter in more depth; however, we have seen already the impact of these meaningful relationships on young children and their ability to develop skills needed to support their future development.

Of course, this is not an exhaustive list of the characteristics of 2-year-olds or their many differing temperaments and personalities; however, we have explored some of the most prevalent challenges of working with this age group and ways that practitioners can reflect to ensure that it is always the children, not our own expectations, that remain at the forefront of our practice.

3 What it means to be a creative pre-schooler

In this chapter, we will look at some of the fundamental features of early years experiences for pre-school children and what has influenced the way we organise our pre-schools. We will explore the misconceptions around teaching and learning and why this is important for pre-school children as well as how this relates to the development of the brain between the ages of 3 and 5. We will also look at common themes, such as planning and appropriate behaviour management and consequences for 3-year-olds, the importance of play and the types of play that we can hope to see from children of this age as well as the vital skills that children need to succeed and become creative thinkers, such as resilience and perseverance, and how we can promote these in the context of their creative experiences whilst respecting children and their development and keeping them interested and motivated.

In the UK, it is largely acknowledged that a pre-school-age child is any child between the ages of 3 years old and starting primary school, which is the term after they turn 4 in most circumstances, although it is worth noting that compulsory school age here in the UK is the term after a child's fifth birthday. This chapter will look specifically at 3- to 5-year-olds in terms of how creativity manifests itself at this age and the routines and rhythms of the day in early years settings that can ensure children are given the skills and allowed the time they need to develop creative thinking whilst ensuring that they are being challenged to think at a level

DOI: 10.4324/9781003271710-5

appropriate to them. As mentioned in the previous chapter, some early years settings combine younger children from the age of 2 with older 3- and 4-year-olds in pre-schools or day nurseries. Many points that have and will be raised in the chapters that follow are applicable to all children within this age range. Most of what we looked at in Chapter 2 can also apply to those children who are considered pre-school age. It is still important to look carefully at transitions and how they are managed and the way in which we speak to young children and converse with them to develop their vocabulary and understanding.

Brain development

Before we delve into the elements that support development of creativity in pre-school children, it is important to consider the developing brain and the changes that occur around the age of 3. We know from research that what happens during the first five years of life are vital prerequisites to future life chances and the experiences we offer children, and the environment they encounter can have a huge impact on these.

Creativity, as we have seen, is a complicated concept and one that is much debated. Whether or not it can be taught or encouraged by adults, whether we support its development when working with young children or whether it is something children are born with is a matter of opinion, and individual thoughts will vary greatly depending on who you speak to. The key thing to remember here is that creativity is vital for future society. Whilst we cannot begin to know what professions will exist in the future and we cannot, therefore, plan what children will need to know, we can give them the best possible start by providing rich experiences and environments and supporting them in the development of key skills that will not age. Skills such as the ability to solve problems independently, think of ideas and resolve conflict without aggression. To think creatively, children need to be given the opportunity to think for themselves, to choose their own ways of doing things; and all this needs to happen in an enabling environment with trusting adults.

Contextualising the coronavirus pandemic

The pre-school years are a time of rapid growth, but children need stimulation, strong relationships and a varied environment and day-to-day interactions with others in order to grow and ensure this rapid growth takes place. We have seen in recent years a decline in children's independent skills, self-care and communication and language, particularly in pre-school-age children. The coronavirus pandemic that swept the globe in 2020 meant that many children left early years education and spent prolonged periods of time at home. The social isolation took its toll on everyone, groups were suspended and opportunities to get out into the world were limited, but it is our children who appear to have suffered the most. With no opportunities for social inter-action with their peers outside the home, months of missed intergenerational relationships and an increase in parents working from home and potentially homeschooling siblings, parents did what they thought was best. Increased periods of time in front of televisions, iPads and other technological devices that temporarily ensured the children were entertained whilst parents worked meant that not all children had the interaction and engagement they would have had if they attended early years settings. Whilst most early years provision remained open throughout the pandemic, only select groups were entitled to attend, and even then, if parents were anxious or at home working, they opted to keep their children with them.

For many children, this was a time to spend with their parents that they would not have got. A time for connecting and being outdoors in nature. For others, it meant prolonged screen time, social iso-lation and potentially volatile households made more so by the circumstances. At the time of writing, the impact of the pan-demic and numerous lockdowns in the UK is becoming more and more apparent. Across the early years sector and education in general, we are seeing a rise in children who lack basic skills, including self-care and feeding, as well as a rise in those with com-munication difficulties and special educa-tional needs. This is thought to be because parents couldn't attend baby groups, toddler groups and extra-curricular activities, such as swimming and other clubs. Children have been away from their peers, so their social skills are also not as developed, and even children who we know can communicate effectively find it difficult to talk to their peers in group situations. This means early years staff are spending more time showing

children how to behave amongst their peers and modelling social behaviour, behaviour which they would almost certainly be aware of had they had contact with adults and peers from birth.

It has always been the role of the practitioner to model behaviour, support children and extend their language and communication; in a sense, this has not changed. The difference, as we are beginning to see it in a post-pandemic world, is children simply don't have age-appropriate skills. Children of 4 are unable to feed themselves because during the pandemic, they were at home being fed. They haven't, therefore, developed the skill most children have by the time they are 2 and a half. We are seeing an increase in children unable to dress themselves or use the toilet independently because whilst they were at home, parents had the time to dress them, and it was easier and quicker to do it for them. In itself, these present as small issues that can be rectified with encouragement; after all, at 3 and 4, children certainly have the dexterity to manage a fork. The problems arise not in the issues themselves but the scale. Whilst one or two children who need extra support is manageable and expected at this age, a group of more than twelve 3- and 4-year-olds who all need extra support with

fundamental skills, such as toileting, feeding and dressing, becomes a difficult feat for even the most seasoned practitioner with years of experience. There is much more expected of early years practitioners now than there was. Add in the support we must also provide to parents as we try to educate them with advice and strategies to support their children at home and in the setting, it has the ability to exhaust practitioners beyond what should be acceptable, no doubt contributing to difficulties with staff recruitment and retention.

In order to work through these difficulties, practitioners need to use what they know about child development to provide experiences and opportunities for children to practise these skills and work with families to share strategies to support their children. We know how important the first five years are, and often, parents need advice and support to understand how what we do in their early years can have an impact on their development.

Self-regulation

We know that children are not born with the ability to self-regulate. Babies cannot manage their emotions and use crying to illicit a response from adults in order to get their needs met. It is then the job of the adult, whether that is a child's parent or an early years practitioner, to establish what they can do to at any given time to support the child when they need it. The same can be said about toddlers and older children. Whilst in many cases, a child's ability to communicate improves rapidly within their third year, there will inevitably be times where they get frustrated, have unmet needs or simply want to exert authority over a situation, often resulting in feelings of anger which may or may not result in an outburst of emotion that they cannot control. This is normal and is all part of a child's ever-changing brain and developmental connections; what is more important is our response to it. Children cannot be expected to regulate their behaviours without first experiencing co-regulation, 'the supportive, guiding process between two individuals and the strategies used in this process to help regulate the child's emotional responses' (Conkbayir, 2022:2).

Being able to consistently regulate their own feelings and behaviour is a major task for a young child and co-regulation is integral to this process, providing them with a healthy blueprint of how to respond to and overcome triggers. A child who has become distressed or dysregulated *needs* adult support to help regulate limbic stress-behaviours.

(Conkbayir, 2020:2)

In terms of what this means for creativity, without strong relationships between children and practitioners, their ability to develop appropriate strategies that are required to think independently and have their own ideas is severely limited, something that is vital for the development of creativity in children. Leaders in early years must, therefore, take steps to ensure all those who work with young children understand the impact of emotional stressors and how they can support children in developing strategies to overcome big emotions. It must also be embedded in practice and evident in all interactions between children and adults. The way we respond to children gives them a subconscious message about how we feel towards them and their behaviour at a given time. In order for children to feel valued, have a sense of belonging and, therefore, able to feel safe, staff must set aside the unwanted behaviour and look towards reducing the trigger and stressors that initiated the response.

Boundaries and consequences

Children learn how to behave by watching others. We have seen how they regularly imitate what they have observed and will often mimic those around them. The same can be said of unwanted behaviours. Children are very aware of what happens around them, perhaps more so than some parents and practitioners would like to believe. In addition to the complex concept of self-regulation and the importance of co-regulation in early years interactions, it is important to ensure that children have the consistency they thrive on when approaching unwanted behaviours. This is particularly important in our interactions with children from the age of 3 who, as well as developing a strong sense of autonomy, also continue to test boundaries and expectations and find their way within their immediate family and community. Children at this age are learning about the world in a very physical hands-on way; they may have matured away from some of the typical behaviours we see in younger children and start to be influenced by those around them as they make and forge friendships with their peers.

In my setting, children learn consequences naturally from an early age; we use china cups from 18 months, and they learn if they throw or drop them, they break. There is no need for adults to impose a consequence on the child because it happened naturally, and they are less likely to throw it again because they can clearly see what happens when they do. This also works in other areas of provision without the need for stringent behaviour management strategies. If adults working with young children understand how to approach situations with the idea of natural consequences in mind and ensure that they treat each child as an individual, they will be better able to work through difficulties and challenges with children in a mutually responsive and respectful way.

A great way to introduce the concept of natural consequences is by introducing more authentic resources into your environment (something we will discuss further in Chapter 7). By using breakables, children will be much quicker to learn fundamental values such as respect and care as well as natural consequences. If a child throws a plastic jug, it won't break; this is probably why lots of settings still insist on using them. This teaches a child that they can throw it if they want and nothing will happen. There are no natural consequences for this action other than perhaps a word of caution or a well-meaning 'please don't throw the jug'. Depending on your settings behaviour policy, this may be enough or, indeed, all you can do. Let's reflect, though, on the probability of the child throwing it again. In my experience, the chances are quite high. It didn't break the first time and it won't break the second time, so why

not do it again. The same can be said for any other toys or resources that are unbreakable. Usually, these are the resources that are plastic, hardwearing and not easily broken. Many settings still use plastic for these very reasons; they don't have to be replaced very often as damage is minimal.

Children need consistent boundaries that mean something to them and are relevant. Stickers and other tangible rewards can send the wrong message to children, yet many settings continue to use behaviour charts and sticker charts for toileting without considering the impact on children. There is nothing wrong with praise if used appropriately and for the right reasons, but it is important to consider that often, children's experiences of rewards at home will be in the form of stickers or a treat and used as bribery, as many parents believe it will make their child behave better. In fact, it creates the opposite. Children who are overexposed to stickers and rewards for behaviour are often the ones who lack intrinsic motivation to behave well. They are not behaving well because it's the right thing to do, they are doing it for what they get out of it, and whilst this may seem trivial at 3, what happens when stickers are no longer interesting? Behaviour inevitably deteriorates, and parents are forced to come up with bigger and better rewards. Whilst this may seem like it is not our concern, we must support children in developing empathy and considering others if we are to increase their intrinsic motivation to do what's right. We can also, where it is wanted, provide support for those parents who may be finding their child's behaviour difficult and offer strategies that don't use extrinsic rewards. The same can be said about praise, often used by parents and practitioners to control a child's behaviour in the short term much the same as stickers. The problem with this is that children then become dependent on rewards and praise; they become unable to think for themselves and often seek reassurance for every idea they have. Seeking approval and developing an inability to make their own choices without the reassurance of others has a devastating effect on early creative thinking since the most important element in its development is the ability to have new ideas and try them out.

The key to a good behaviour management strategy is one that is embedded in the culture of a setting, not a written policy laminated and placed in every room so practitioners know what to do in a range of situations. This includes the language we use around sharing, turn taking and conflict resolution, something that young children can find difficult without support. Even though we know this as a method of best practice, why then do we hear calls of 'sharing is caring' from well-meaning practitioners? Children need to be supported when learning acceptable social behaviour and just because a child says sharing is caring, it doesn't necessarily mean the child who wants it gets it. It is the subliminal messages we send children that matter. Yes, to take turns and share is kind, but only when a child is developmentally able is this appropriate. Children can be encouraged using sand timers or given a certain limit such as riding the bike around the track three times before it is the next child's turn. We must be careful as practitioners to use language in a meaningful way rather than learnt phrases that young children pick up on and simply repeat to get their own way.

Another example of a common phrase that many practitioners are guilty of using with young children to ensure they are following particular rules is using 'walking feet' or 'kind hands'. Let's reflect on the absurdity of these sentences when talking to children. We all know we have two hands and two feet. We use our feet for running, walking, jumping, skipping and a range of other actions, children can't swap and change their feet depending on the action required. Instead of confusing children with phrases like these, we should be encouraging children to identify areas that are safe to run and those places where walking is best (such as indoors). Conflict amongst children is a crucial area of development as children gain understanding of others and themselves and as a result, they learn strategies for co-operation. Simply telling a child to use their 'kind hands' does nothing to support their understanding of others' emotions, perspectives or how to respond when they feel upset or angry.

Children need boundaries and clear expectations to thrive, but do not confuse it with punishment and rewards. They test the limits of the adults around them so that we can show them 'patience, love and discipline' (Bottrill, 2018:17). Children need us to model what these behaviours look like in challenging situations so that they can build the skills and understanding they need to use them in the future. All settings should have a clear strategy in place based on what they want for children and what they know about child development. There is no one-size-fits-all for young children, and what works for one may not work for another, even if the situation is the same.

Agency

The idea of agency in early years goes hand in hand with the behavioural expectations we have of young children. As we have seen, a key feature of creativity and its development in early years is the ability of children to make choices. When we think about children and their ability to be curious, imaginative and social from birth, we often forget that in order to develop these skills further, we need to give children the ability to act and make choices for themselves. The subject of children's *agency*, which for the purpose of this book has been defined as the 'quality which enables a person to initiate intentional action' (Mashford-Scott & Church, 2011:17), is one that has caused tension in recent years but is a vital component for children to develop the skills required for creative thinking. Despite the growing interest in young children's education from a political and social standpoint (Mashford-Scott et al., 2012:231), this tension focusses on 'the extent to which young children can be considered to possess agency' (Mashford-Scott & Church, 2011:17) and is guided by the 'ambivalence and ambiguity in understanding and accepting children's participatory rights' (Berthelsen & Brownlee, 2005:4).

There are several authors who discuss the capabilities of pre-school children and those in primary school and beyond, particularly in terms of agency in varying social contexts. As Page (cited in Hirst & Nutbrown, 2005:93) adds, 'work with children under three is an area which has largely been neglected', and through compiling my background research for this book, it is abundantly clear that young children and their ability to become active agents in their environment and, subsequently, act accordingly has indeed been somewhat overlooked. There are several reasons for this, with many writers suggesting work with younger children can be difficult due to research methods and their perceived inability to give consent. There are others who will blame young children's lack of communicative ability in their early years, making any evidence collected somewhat fragmented. Whatever the reason, it is clear that young children are underrepresented in certain areas of research, and despite the growing spotlight on a child's first five years, there remains much to be done to ensure that they are heard and listened to for their contributions.

Teaching and learning

There is a tendency among practitioners, especially those working with pre-school-aged children, to use the terms *teaching* and *learning* almost interchangeably; however, it is important to note that the two are not the same and can have very different connotations depending on who you speak to. For many, teaching is something that happens in schools. Whilst this is presumed to be the case, it can be said that early years practitioners are teachers, too; the only thing that changes is the age of the child. It is important to briefly touch on this as there is much debate about what our pre-school children *should* know and what knowledge we expect of them between the ages of 3 and 5, with a focus in many pre-schools on school readiness as they reach 4.

A common practice among early years provision is the inclusion of themes and topics to plan activities for young children to participate in. We know that this is not the most effective way for children to learn new concepts or ideas. Many settings still use the approach as a way to ensure they are teaching a variety of topics and what they believe to be relevant knowledge, therefore, learning, about a particular subject. For example, it may be transport week with children learning about buses, cars, aeroplanes and boats; there will no doubt be themed books, toys and laminated signs designed to teach children, ensuring that practitioners can complete their planning paperwork and tick a box that tells them they have completed transport week. The following week, it may be the solar system, colours or minibeasts, all with a set of resources, books and accompanying sheets to complete.

Whilst this may work for some settings, it is unclear just how much is done for the practitioners benefit and how much is for the children. The main problem with planning this way is that it doesn't mean anything to the children. Themes are decided by well-meaning practitioners who then spend time thinking of and preparing activities for children around the theme they have chosen. The joy of working with children is seeing the world through their eyes, seeing what is important to them and what they enjoy, and then finding ways to extend and develop their ideas, not ours. We know that if children are not interested, they are less engaged and, more importantly, less likely to retain any new information. Planning should, therefore, focus on the child and what is relevant to them. Many settings have moved on from topic planning and found a new way that keeps the child and their interests at the centre of everything they do. Reflections Small School in Worthing focus on enquiry-based learning with their pre-school children, an approach that instils a love of learning from a young age and ensures that children remain focussed and highly motivated.

Since the inception of the early years foundation stage, practitioners have followed a somewhat tick list–type planning format, ensuring that children were hitting particular markers at certain times and were mindful of the ages and stages of development. We will discuss further the impact of Piaget's ideas on current early years practices in Chapter 4, as they remain very much relevant to today's early years curriculums; however, more recently, and particularly with the revised early years foundation stage framework in 2021, practitioners are being encouraged to move beyond age restrictions for milestones and trust their own judgement in terms of what the children they care for need. There are, of course, certain milestones that all children will achieve. All children, unless there is a special educational need or disability that prevents it, will learn to roll, walk and eventually put together words and form sentences. The important difference here is the rate and timing that they occur. Whilst some children may be walking on or before their first birthday, it can take others until closer to 18 months to 2 years to fully master the skill, and we know that most children use sounds and babble to communicate in infancy; by the time a child is 2, we would expect them to have a repertoire of words they use and even more that they understand, but this is not the case for all children, and some may take much longer to produce single words and sentences.

There is also a very real question about the assessment of children in the UK. With practitioners concerned with paperwork and the need to ensure that children display school readiness by the time they leave pre-school, there is a mismatch between what the role of the adult is and what it should be. Sara Meadows's example in her book *The Child as a Thinker* can provide a useful analogy of what the modern–day curriculum seems to have developed children into. She writes, 'brains just are not simple straight in/straight out machines where one thing leads rigidly to another' (Meadows, 2006:321); perhaps this can explain some of the more contemporary issues facing education where children are merely part of a wider system. Unable to express their views and continuing to be done to, instead of with, limiting their agentic behaviour and subsequent creative thinking that may have emerged.

Meador states that 'creativity . . . declines when children enter Kindergarten, at around the age of five or six' (1992:164). In a UK context, this would refer to primary school–age children who would be entering year 1, having already been in formal education for a year, as in many European countries, children start formal education much later, often attending kindergartens before starting school. It can, however, still be applied, as it means if this statement were true, the focus should also be on teachers in primary schools (particularly teaching those in reception), as they may not be doing enough to support children and encourage this creative ability which begins to decline by age 5 or 6.

Planning for pre-school

This must all be considered when planning for any child with the focus being on meeting them where they are and not where practitioners believe they should be. As young children develop more mature skills and abilities, it is vital that they are challenged to come up with and explore their own ideas and ways of working. The most crucial part of planning for pre-school-age children is knowing them. What they like, what they are interested in and what fascinates them. This can then be used to support and further their learning. Ensuring that we stay true to the children and are guided by what is relevant to them will mean they will be more likely to engage, and not only that, but stay engaged for prolonged periods of time as well as begin to participate in sustained shared thinking and develop the ability to ask questions and comment on what interests them.

Abbie-May Moore encourages practitioners at her setting to use the seasons to invoke curiosity in young children and encourage them to ask questions.

As the seasons change, we look to nature as our guide for invitations to play. For experiences and opportunities to explore. We are careful not to get sucked back into the theme or topic of Halloween, by filling our environments with plastic from the £1 shop, by adding spiders and cobwebs to children's play spaces. Instead, we celebrate Autumn, golden leaves and falling seeds, not the topic of Halloween. We go with children's thinking and ideas, and step away from a 'planned topic' for the month. At Scallywags, we follow the seasons and celebration of the natural world, allowing children to feel empowered and confident and become the capable and competent learners who experience the natural environment through active exploration, curiosity, awe and wonder.

Asking questions to develop children's critical thinking and creativity is crucial, but practitioners must be mindful that this can sometimes cause anxiety for children. Knowledge of the children you work with will enable you to approach each child in a way that respects their individuality and gives them the opportunity and time to process what is being asked. Planning in the moment, a style of planning where practitioners focus on extending children's play in the moment rather than pre-planning, supports the idea that in order to develop creativity, children need the opportunity to discover their own interests and extend them with the support and guidance of mindful adults. Often, this style of planning involves leaving the environment and continuous provision for children to investigate on their own terms or providing simple provocations to excite children and offer new ideas based on their existing interests.

At my setting, we have taken elements of different planning styles to suit the cohort of children we have, providing high-quality experiences and interactions without compromising the children by having to complete lengthy paperwork or gather children unnecessarily for group time. We view planning as a collaborative endeavour, keeping children at the forefront of our daily experiences. We have adopted many of the principles of planning in the moment and combined them with the floor book approach to planning with young children. This combination has seen a huge increase in the participation of young children, as we use their existing knowledge to pose questions about what they want to find out about, creating enquiries and projects that are meaningful to the children.

The practitioner added pans for the children to mix their creations.

SENSORY EXPLORATION

Using bicarbonate of soda, vinegar, orange paint & glitter the children made fizzing potions.

Today we spent some time engaged in a sensory experience, led by our interest in texture

The children were offered lime jelly, cooked spaghetti, cornflour & small insects to explore freely. After some hesitation, the children made 'witches brew'

Jelly Mixes

Tabitha made a jelly mix using lime jelly, oats, cornflour & water. She then added ants & spiders.

"I'M MIXING FOR THE WITCH"

When Asia said she was scared, we decided to collect the spiders in a potion bottle and put a lid on to keep them safe.
"I'M SCARED- THE SPIDERS" ASIA

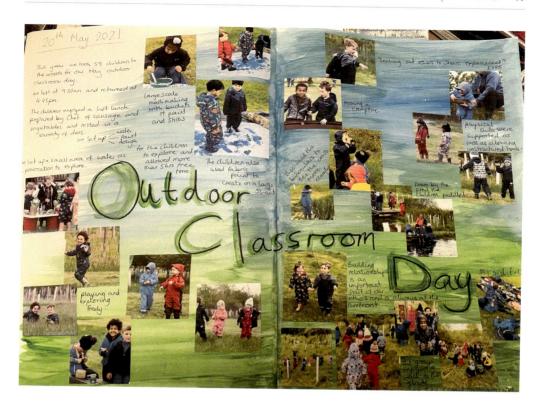

This means that some of their day is guided but not directed by adults. The difference here is a noticeable one. At Wally's, we value the child as knowledgeable and capable in their own endeavours. As they reach 3 and 4, children's skills increase, their fine motor and gross motor control is developing rapidly, and they benefit from the guidance of an adult to expand what they know and show them how to use different materials and techniques. For us, this takes the format of adult-guided project or enquiry sessions. We use these to introduce new concepts and techniques with the children and explore different ways of doing things through collaboration. We use this time to reflect on what we know and want to find out as well as what the children are interested in so that we can provide opportunities for sustained shared thinking and learning.

These sessions take many forms, usually with materials that the children don't have access to all the time. They work in small groups with an adult and explore a variety of concepts and ideas, all whilst working collaboratively. This could include sharing new art techniques, such as inking or batik as well as woodwork projects, sculpture, and modelling. We also use the opportunity in these small groups to return to our floor book and reflect on our projects, what we have done and if we could do anything differently, instilling some of the elements of creativity and critical thinking from a young age. Children learn they are respected, are listened to and, perhaps most importantly, belong to the group, and children learn that their ideas hold value amongst their peers and the adults who work with them. We do not set objectives, and sessions are based on our child-centred pedagogy, ensuring that we are sharing our knowledge through some of the hundred languages of children.

> A child-led approach is wild and free, it roams from minute to minute, hour to hour, day to day, sometimes veering off, sometimes simple, sometimes brilliant, sometimes soaring, often taking you to places you could never imagine: always exciting, always something different, forever changing, never standing still.
>
> (Bottrill, 2018:10)

Play and essential skills

There is certainly a lot to think about when working with pre-school children, and most of it, as practitioners, we do subconsciously. We are continuously reflecting on our practice, how we listen to children and plan for them, and how we respond in times where there may be challenges. The answer to almost all our concerns and questions about young children in this age range is play. Play and connection can solve even the most difficult of situations and must be given the respect and place in our settings it deserves.

Play is a fundamental of early years practice. It is what many of us live and breathe. Constantly thinking about how we can support the children and extend their ideas through meaningful engagement and invitations to find out about the world, children need uninterrupted, long periods of time to play. They collaborate with others and engage on deeper levels, often developing skills such as conflict resolution and resilience, too. As we have mentioned, this can be something that leaders in early years fail to recognise as more and more periods of the day, particularly for pre-school children, is spent preparing for formal education. Phonics sessions, circle time, time to talk; whatever name you give it, the outcome is still the same. Prolonged periods of time sitting, listening (or not) to the adult attempting to teach what are, to the children, abstract concepts, irrelevant to their lived experience.

Play at its heart is creativity. It is the opportunity to take resources and ideas and combine them with as many elements as the child chooses to create something new and meaningful to them. Children from 3, perhaps more than most, need time to play, as their pre-school years draw to a close near their fourth birthday and they make the transition into formal education, so their opportunities for free play decline, too. This should not be the case, but sadly, the education system in this country is designed with a top-down approach to teaching young children. Viewing them almost as empty containers to be filled by learning information by rote in order to pass a phonics screening or SATS. It is our role in early years to give children as much time to play as we possibly can, taking into account mealtimes, opportunities for rest and other transitional times in the day. The end of play comes to all of us, as adults; we won't recall the day or even month we stopped playing, but slowly, throughout our childhood and the imposition of schooling, play was less and less important and was quickly replaced by sitting at desks and completing worksheets. We need to do what we can now to protect childhood and allow children the chance to play for as long as we can.

> Play creates the conditions for children to test the world, to make sense of it, to grow the skills needed to communicate, to negotiate and express their inner selves . . . Real play that is accepting of children's voices and need for freedom to make them heard; and real play that is not encumbered by the adult world.
>
> (Bottrill, 2018:29)

For those of us in home provision, nurseries and pre-schools, we cannot control what happens beyond the fifth year, when children leave our settings and start reception. We hope that they have the chance to continue to play, to explore and discover a new world of possibilities, but as the years slowly go by, these opportunities get fewer and fewer. It is absolutely crucial then that we do as much playing as we can whilst we can, to give children the skills they will need as they grow.

4 Pioneering influences

This chapter will focus on some of the theorists who have shaped the way we think about early years and, more specifically, our work with those children who fall into the category of toddlers and pre-school children. I have already discussed some of the founding theories of early years, including the work of Maria Montessori, Rudolph Steiner and Friedrich Froebel in my first book *Discover Creativity with Babies* (2021); and here, we will explore some more of the important individuals who continue to shape our work with young children, such as Erik Erikson, Susan Isaacs and John Dewey, and how they have stood the test of time and impacted our practice. We will also revisit the Reggio Emilia pre-schools of Italy and Montessori practice with toddlers and older children.

Most settings here in the UK have a high proportion of qualified practitioners; with the government pushing a graduate-led workforce, some settings are lucky enough to have one or more members of staff with degrees, early years professional status or even postgraduate studies in the field of early years. In line with the early years foundation stage, settings including childminders and other types of provision are required to be aware of the statutory ratios that are in place when considering recruiting more staff. The rules surrounding ratios for early years, defined by the level of qualifications an individual has, are in place to ensure not only that our children are safe in their provision but that those caring for them have sound knowledge of child development and behaviour. It would stand to reason then that when we discuss the pioneering theories and thinkers who have influenced our practice and continue to do so in many ways, most practitioners will know who we mean. Sadly, this is not always the case, and this can create problems within settings when staff don't know or understand why they have a particular vision or set of values, making it difficult for them to embed them within their practice.

Our view of the child

The most important element among the theory is the child. The view of the child we hold will determine which set of values we hold closest and will be reflected in the way we organise our curriculum and what we provide for children daily as well as our expectations of them. It is

DOI: 10.4324/9781003271710-6

important to remember that these views will also reflect our personal experiences. How we were brought up, the environment and the places we have been, all impact the way we think about children and how we care for them.

Ashley Corcoran knows how important it is to keep children at the heart of our pedagogy and uses the knowledge she gained from her teaching degree and what she knows about the pioneers of early childhood to influence her own setting, Love of Learning Child Care.

> I believe that young children do not get enough time, space or opportunity to simply be young children. Instead of using my teaching degree to do more of the same, I decided to use my knowledge of what children really need and put it into my practice. The kids are my inspiration, my motivation and their needs are what keep me innovating.

Children are born curious, eager to learn about the world and wanting of social connection. They are not waiting to be filled with knowledge, nor should they be talked at in the hope that we can impart wisdom and prepare them for life as an adult. They are human beings with valuable thoughts, feelings and ideas about how to spend their time and who to spend it with and should be viewed as such. Unfortunately, in this country, we have an education system that appears to have forgotten the work of many theorists who spent years developing their ideas with the children at the heart. Instead, we have created a culture, particularly in 3- and 4-year-old provision, where staff are observed sitting with groups of children and teaching them colours, the weather, days of the week and about pre-planned topics they have no interest in.

If we take the view that children are strong, capable and knowledgeable and need to learn through opportunities and experiences, why are we continuing to teach the weather indoors on a carpet? Why are we attempting to have 3- and 4-year-olds recite the days of the week? Why are we spending time asking children to learn numbers by rote? All these things are irrelevant to children and will not help or support them with what they should actually be finding out about. We are surprised when our cohort have limited social skills; this is because we didn't give them time to interact with others freely. We are surprised when they have limited attention and listening skills; this is because they spend too much time listening (or not) to adults talk about things that don't interest them. We are surprised when children don't like getting muddy, wet or dirty; this is because we were too busy telling them about the weather rather than experiencing it. This is having a massive detrimental effect on our young children, being full of questions but learning not to ask them.

This is particularly relevant when we consider the term *school readiness*. When we think about how children are prepared for starting primary school, the earlier examples ring alarmingly true. Many settings have a school readiness programme that encourages carpet time, phonics, number lessons and various other activities meant to replicate what it will be like in a classroom. The main problem with this is we have children who are 3 and 4 years old, and they are not developmentally ready to sit for long periods in a circle, crossing their legs and listening. There are lots of ways we can support children through the transition to school, but above all else, we need to keep in mind the theories of the pioneers who advocated for play and interaction with others. Only this will ensure that children are indeed ready to start school.

Little Learners in Corby prides itself on the relationships that staff build with the children they care for. Knowing them well and ensuring that they feel valued are important features of their pedagogy. This also supports their understanding of what the children need in terms of their development, and responsive practitioners are always there with thoughtful interactions.

Play is a fundamental building block of all development in young children; it is in play that they learn how to problem-solve, how to collaborate, how to interact with others appropriately and what to do if something doesn't go their way. No other stage in life is prepared for, and neither should school be. We don't prepare ourselves for adulthood before we get there, and we certainly don't prepare ourselves to be in a residential care home by staying home in an armchair. I wonder then why there is still such pressure on early years provision to ensure children are prepared for school. Practitioners should instead be facilitating play, meeting the needs of the children and ensuring that they provide an environment that supports all areas of development in an age-appropriate way. We need to instil a can-do attitude, we need to provide physical activities to promote muscle strength and growth, and most importantly, we need to ensure that children are confident, curious and able to communicate effectively with others so that they can make friends and resolve conflict when it arises. This is what is important to 3- and 4-year-olds.

Pioneering influences

Children learn in a variety of ways; through the right environment and interaction with adults, they will make progress. We know about child development through the writing, philosophies and theories of many individuals spanning over one hundred years. I have outlined subsequently some of whom I believe to be the pioneers of early years pedagogy and practice as well as briefly explored some alternative curriculums from that of the early years foundation stage. Whilst this is, of course, not an exhaustive list, it does feature those who I believe have made an impact that is such that we can still see elements of it in practice today. I have also revisited some of the thinkers outlined in my first book, as I believe them to be an integral part of the way we think about children and what they are capable of in today's society.

John Dewey (1859–1952)

John Dewey's greatest contribution to modern early years practice is the now widely accepted notion that children learn through experiences and through their interests. He also was the first to develop the notion of reflective professional practice. Something that we all use in early years as professionals.

Society at the time had assumed that children were passive learners, had to be filled with knowledge and had little of value to share. Dewey's theory directly opposed this and suggested that children were able to be active participants in learning. This was especially the case when adults and children worked together; this, he suggested, was when the most valuable learning occurred.

Although he was critical of many child-led approaches at the time, this was because, for him, the role of the adult was not of importance in these early models of child-led curriculums. He asserted that the teacher should be seen as the 'intellectual leader of a social group' (Dewey, cited in Pound, 2011:22). He believed that children were more than individuals and that their curiosity could be stimulated by social contact. Similar to the idea of cultural capital that we have embedded in modern-day early years, Dewey believed that schools should help children develop the skills they need to be part of society.

It is easy to see how much of what Dewey theorised about childhood and development holds true today. More and more settings are adopting ways of planning in the moment, giving value to the ideas and interests of the children, and allowing them to decide what and how they play and learn. Practitioners in this method are also of high value as they carefully observe and then provide ways for children to extend their learning, just as Dewey outlined.

Susan Isaacs (1885–1948)

Influenced by Dewey, Susan Isaacs was a psychologist whose theory of child development focussed on the importance of play and how children learn through social interaction with others. She advocated for children making their own choices and asserted that play has 'the greatest value for the child when it is really free and his own' (Isaacs, 1929:133). Isaacs also placed great value on the role of the practitioner and the environment. She believed that early years education should be something every child goes through, and whilst it can't replace the home environment, it can be an extension of it. This is reflected in many modern-day models of early years pedagogy as more and more nurseries and pre-schools do their best to create a home from a home-style environment.

It is this environment, like the Reggio Emilia approach that originated in Italy, that has an impact on the child. She believed that children should have access to a wide range of resources that suited their ability, and this extends to the outdoor environment, too, which should have elements of risk and challenge for all children. Adults in Susan Isaacs's theory are very important. They have a huge role to play in supporting young children and ensuring that they feel safe and valued, and that they are afforded the time they need to play. This is something that we still strive for in our settings today. That children are happy in their environment and are able to choose their own resources and engage with others through access to free play are things we must thank Isaacs for.

Maria Montessori (1870–1952)

> To be independent is to be able to do things for yourself, to be able to make your own choices and to be able to manage the consequences of those choices on your own.
>
> (Maria Montessori)

The key to Maria Montessori's approach to early years when working with young children is the notion that children are constantly and repeatedly saying to the adults around them, 'help me to do it for myself' (Montessori, 1949/1982:136). Montessori believed that children were capable of amazing things, often uncharacteristic of their age. The cornerstone of her approach is having independence and teaching children how to do things instead of doing it for them. Montessori philosophy also puts high value on teaching children life skills, such as cooking, gardening and helping to clean the environments; this ensures that children are equipped with a range of skills that will allow them to develop their independence. There are also some very specific resources that are commonplace not only in Montessori-based provision but in other settings, too. Often, they are made of wood and all with the intention of allowing children to develop their own ideas and learn vital concepts.

Almost all settings are striving for independent children who can manage themselves in a range of situations and carry out tasks without unnecessary adult support. These ideas are almost certainly underpinned by Montessori's theory of child development and how we ensure we are giving children the chance to learn how to do things for themselves.

Lev Vygotsky (1896–1934)

Just as we will revisit the work and theory of Malaguzzi, I felt it important to recap the importance of Vygotsky on modern-day early years when working with toddlers and pre-school children. Whilst he had well-known ideas and theories about the development of children from birth, we will briefly discuss those aspects of his theory that can be applied to children from 2 in practice today.

As well as the notion that children develop in a social world, his work focussed on play, language and the well-known term *Zone of Proximal Development* (ZPD). We know that children develop through their experience of the social world. This is well documented, and we know how important it is for children to be exposed to a language-rich and social environment. We also know the impact on a child's future life chances that not having prolonged social contact has on young children's language development through extensive research. For Vygotsky, 'the very mechanism underlying higher mental functions is a copy from social interaction' (Vygotsky, 1988:74).

Play was seen by Vygotsky as important because he believed it was in play that children acted beyond what they were perceived to be capable of. This is important, as more modern-day pedagogy focusses on play and children choosing how to spend their time. In the context of this book, it is vital that children have time to play uninterrupted as they learn so much more by directing their own play and extending their ideas with others in a social context. This is where the Zone of Proximal Development can also be seen as important, not only for the children but for the adults that work with them, too. ZPD describes the gap between what a child can do on their own and what they can achieve with the help of another person. This is a great way to consider how we support young children and scaffold their learning. Practitioners must first mindfully observe; only then can we know what it is that the child can achieve independently. Then when the opportunity arises for support, practitioners must ensure they challenge the child to think just beyond what they are capable of on their own, thus making sure they were working 'at a level that was optimal for stimulating children's development' (Keenan & Evans, 2009:45).

Erik Erikson (1902–1994)

Erik Erikson was a developmental psychologist best known for his psychosocial theory, describing different stages that humans go through to develop within a social world. Beginning at birth, there are eight stages, according to Erikson. Starting in infancy, he asserts that through each stage, human beings have a conflict they must overcome; 'these were believed to lead to the dynamic forces which produce change and development' (Pound, 2011:64). As this book focusses primarily on children aged 2 to 5, we will look briefly at stages 2 and 3. From the age of 18 months until a child is 3, they go through what he called autonomy vs. shame and doubt. Success here will lead to the virtue of will. It makes sense that between the age of 1 and 3, children begin to develop their independence. According to Erikson, this is vital, and if encouraged, they will benefit from increased confidence, become more independent and have higher levels of self-esteem. If parents and adults caring for young children do not nurture their autonomy at this stage, children can become dependent on others and lack the self-esteem and confidence to try new things. The aim has to be 'self-control without a loss of self-esteem' (Gross and Humphreys, 1992:98).

The next stage, for children between 3 and 5, is that of initiative vs. guilt. As we know, children can become assertive as they try to control their surroundings and begin to dominate others in their play and at home; what happens here forms the basis of social awareness. Children, according to Erikson, need to be given the opportunity to choose what to do, who to play with as well as how to initiate their own play. If they are not given these opportunities, they will begin to feel a sense of guilt, and too much guilt can make the child slow to interact with others and will inhibit their creativity.

We can see, using Erikson's theory of development, that it still holds true for our practice today. Erikson states it is critical that adults allow children to explore the limits of their abilities within an encouraging environment which is tolerant of failure, something which we have seen can be difficult for some practitioners whose automatic reaction is to appease or rescue a child from their distress. It is far better that children are supported in their independent skills to ensure they develop the necessary skills they need to make progress.

Loris Malaguzzi (1920–1994)

I wanted to briefly revisit Loris Malaguzzi and the pre-schools in Reggio Emilia, Italy, as the impact it has had on the way the UK organises its environments and how adults interact with young children is far-reaching. It has led to a huge following in recent years, of early years practitioners who want to embed some of the principles that make their pre-schools so successful. The innovative approach, founded on the notion that child-led is what is best for young children's learning and development, was the work of Loris Malaguzzi, a psychologist.

Malaguzzi's Reggio Emilia style of education was unique in the way that it understood young children are individuals who are independent and are capable. Malaguzzi believed that all children are resourceful and intelligent, and because it is an approach, rather than a method, it is universal in the way that it can be altered to suit any environment or cohort of children as long as the principles remain intact. This is most likely the reason it is so prevalent in the UK and internationally outside of Reggio Emilia. 'Malaguzzi rejected Piaget's stage notions as too limiting. He drew a powerful image of the child, social from birth, full of intelligence, curiosity, and wonder' (Edwards, 2002:6).

For Malaguzzi, planning (in the sense we know it) must be centred around the child and their interests, and the adults who care for them should facilitate learning during play.

> Teachers follow the children's interests and do not provide focused instruction in reading and writing; however, they foster emergent literacy as children record and manipulate their ideas and communicate with others. The curriculum has purposive progression but not scope and sequence.
>
> (Edwards, 2002:7)

The idea that children are capable individuals is something that is shared by many of the theories we have explored, as is the importance of the environment. The environment plays a pivotal role in children's learning and is referred to as the third teacher. Within their environment, children can work with a range of open-ended resources and natural and recycled materials which stimulate creativity, exploration and imagination. Environments are aesthetically pleasing for both adults and children and are designed as such to ensure children feel a sense of calm, wellbeing and belonging. Many settings now consider themselves Reggio-inspired as they see the value in Malaguzzi's approach and develop their own unique way of embedding it within their practice.

By swapping topics and themes to working in the moment with children, it would seem we are moving closer to what life in a true Reggio Emilia pre-school would look like. An environment of respect, collaboration and infinite creativity.

Putting theories into practice

It is important that the pioneers of early years continue to be taught in colleges and on relevant courses so that new members of staff have a sound knowledge of their theories and ideas, many of which are still extremely valuable to our practice.

In my setting, we take pride in the pedagogy we have developed through the years, reflecting on best practice and being mindful of the children we care for and their needs whilst all the time keeping in mind the ideas of the pioneers. We plan collaboratively, ensuring that the child remains at the centre of our practice, and we carry out projects, providing hands-on experiences that will engage the children and stimulate their thinking. We draw inspiration from nature pedagogy, too, instilling a sense of care for the environment and developing empathy as we go.

In her childminding practice, Imogen Eyre draws inspiration from theory as well as ensures children feel valued and listened to. She uses a range of natural, sensory resources, similar to that described by Steiner.

I believe that creativity is sparked from individuality and the only way children will be brave enough to be their unique self is if we foster an environment and an attitude that promotes safety, love and respect. We care for children from all walks of life, with any number of experiences, cultures and languages and we like to reflect this in our environment and this collection of experiences is what sparks their imaginative play, from small world to large loose part play. We wholeheartedly believe in a play-based approach, where the child is the master of their own learning.

I'm also working through the Hygge in the Early Years accreditation so our approach is heavily based on this, along with elements of Montessori and loose parts practice.

Another setting who has embedded a particular set of values is Nina's Nursery High Lane. Having successfully undertaken the Curiosity Approach accreditation and subsequently becoming a brand ambassador, manager Amanda Redwood and her deputy Charlotte Blackburn know how important it is to reflect the ideas of the pioneers within everyday practice to get the best creative outcomes for young children.

The curriculum provided at Nina's focuses on child led play and, in the moment, learning which is enabled through invitations and provocations to play, most, if not all of these facilitating creativity. The practitioners, referred to in house as Play Partners understand the broad spectrum and unlimited possibilities of creativity, including, music both creating and listening to it alongside dance, creating and inventing in the construction areas utilising real tools, loose parts, lengths of wood, tubing, pipes; through the whole nursery approach, parents are involved with helping to provide items we can repurpose from junk modelling to kitchen tiles.

The artistic side of creativity is supported by areas referred to as Atelier's where children are given the space to let their ideas evolve into masterpieces, these areas are not restricted to tables but instead can be horizontal on walls or chalkboards or laid out across the floor. In a similar way to how resources are not just limited to paint, the child is not limited to a chair but instead can use their whole body in a process of testing and developing ideas free from the constraints of a product premade by an adult with expectations of perfection. Alongside the atypical art supplies of paint, pencils, crayons, and chalk the children also have access to other materials which they can mark make with, mould, and manipulate such as clay, playdough, sand, mud, loose parts all of which are encouraged to engage the children's creative sides to flow freely.

Amanda Calloway ensures her provision remains homely, by providing a calm space and open-ended opportunities, much like the environment suggested by Susan Isaacs.

As a childminder whose own children are grown up it's important to me that my home looks like a home. I like to provide a calm natural play space filled with open ended resources.

Childminders are in a unique position of caring for children in their homes; therefore, it is even more important that their pedagogy is reflected in their provision. Andrea Booth, owner of Andrea's Childcare, uses lots of natural, wooden resources in her setting to evoke a sense of connection to nature.

These examples showcase how good practice involves keeping children at the centre of any reflective changes and experiences. Children learn best from a hands-on approach, through collaboration with others, through the quality and range of resources, and by leaders ensuring all staff share the same values.

5 Forming respectful relationships

A key element of developing creativity in young children is the need for respectful, trusting relationships in early years settings and with those adults who are important and familiar to them. All human relationships are built on respect and trust. This chapter will explore the ways in which we can foster these relationships, the steps that practitioners can take to ensure they provide the right emotional environment for children approaching their third year and how to ensure children up to the age of 5 are given the opportunity to make independent choices about how they spend their time and who they spend it with. I will explore the underlying need for pre-school children to be given space and time, and how this is different to what we afford infants. We will look briefly at the key person approach when working with slightly older children and how these relationships impact how the child expresses themself within a pre-school environment.

Respectful relationships with toddlers

Looking after a 2-year-old is not easy. Anyone who has ever worked with toddlers will tell you it is the most interesting yet challenging stage of development for young children, not least because when a child is 2, they have some of the most ingenious ways to do things that, as an adult, we would never have thought of. Now, imagine a room full of them, perhaps twelve, sixteen or even twenty children, all experiencing the same joys, interests, frustrations and emotional outbursts but yet all at different rates. They get themselves into the tightest of spaces and the funniest of scenarios, and despite often wanting to pull our hair out at the

DOI: 10.4324/9781003271710-7

sight of their latest mischief, we can't help but marvel at their forming personality, their inquisitive nature and their desire to do just about anything they want, regardless of consequences.

Some would argue that the toddler years are the most formative. We know that developmentally, the first five years of a child's life are vital for their overall development, and what happens to them in those years can have a lasting impact on their future life chances. It stands to reason then that parents and those people who have the most contact with young children have a huge responsibility to ensure they get it right in those formative years. The relationships that we build with young children are important for many reasons. Having already established bonds with their parents as babies, as children move towards their third year of life, they are becoming more independent and finding out more about the world around them, and they need the adults in their lives to realise this. One of the biggest barriers to relationships with toddlers is adults' inability to see them as capable and independent human beings. This is not so much practitioners, although some still hold the opinion that children should behave and listen when told (something which is often developmentally inappropriate at this age).

Toddlers are finding their place in the world in the only way they know how, through expressing themselves, often using big emotions. They are trying to control their world as they develop independence, and this is something that parents often don't acknowledge. As babies, they were dependent on their parents and caregivers for everything. In order to thrive, their needs had to be interpreted and then fulfilled often by those closest to them. However, as children begin to explore their autonomy, they often push boundaries and want to do things for themselves, causing problems as parents don't always acknowledge this shift in development. We often see children's unwanted behaviour in settings and, upon speaking to parents, come to realise it is not because they are trying to be difficult or that they are just going through the terrible twos. No, it is because adults closest to the child have failed to recognise their growth. Their desire to move on from bottles at 3 and their behaviour at bedtime are not because they are trying to push their parents' buttons but because they don't want to be in a cot at 3 years old or a highchair to eat. Children learn from those around them; if everyone else is sitting at a table, simply sliding your 3-year-old into a highchair is, of course, more than likely going to result in frustration. It is not that the child isn't hungry; they want to be big and sit at the table. As educators, this is something we recognise; our pre-schools are not places for highchairs and cots, and we treat children as they deserve to be treated. Part of developing respectful and trusting relationships with children is advocating for them. If you become aware that a child is still having a bottle at 4, ask why. There may be a very good reason, but more often than not, parents just haven't realised their children are growing up and need they need the expertise of those working with children to support them.

Building relationships with families

More and more 2-year-olds are finding themselves in childcare settings, whether home-based or in nurseries and pre-schools, as this is the age where parents either feel they are old enough to start their early childhood education, or it may be that parents (particularly mothers) start to think about returning to work. There can be many factors that impact the decision to put a child into a setting, but whatever the reason, it seems that the choice of provision will depend greatly on the needs of the family and the temperament of the child.

If parents choose to send their babies into childcare, they tend to choose a setting based on their own needs and desired characteristics. Whether a setting is close to home and how the parent feels about the staff often impact the choice, and very little concern is given to the child itself – this isn't intentional, but the reason is often that for babies, they are viewed as not yet having their own opinions, or if they do, they can't communicate them effectively enough to impact their parent's decision. As any parent of a 2-year-old will tell you, once they reach an age where they can communicate their intentions and needs effectively, choosing a setting becomes about what a parent perceives their child needs. If they believe their child loves the outdoors, they will look for a setting with a big outdoor area; if they enjoy art, they'll look for somewhere that promotes creative endeavours. This can make choosing a setting difficult and may mean that certain settings are overlooked, despite their high quality, if they don't provide what the parent is looking for.

It's not only the environment that will impact a parent's choice though. The people who work within the setting and, more specifically, those who have direct contact with the child become the focus for many. It is often said that you get a feel for a place from the minute you step through the door; as adults, we get that feeling when we walk into hotels, shops and cafés. We know what it feels like to have a warm atmosphere, an accepting greeting, or we know those places that feel cold and unwelcoming, perhaps the coffee shop where we'd prefer to get a takeaway than sit down. The same is true for different types of early years provision. Not many would be described as unwelcoming (that isn't the nature of the job); however, different places will suit different families, and what one family thinks is fantastic, another may feel is not suited to them or their child.

Respectful relationships with 3–5-year-olds

There are many invisible influences in the environment, such as the way children are welcomed, the way they are encouraged to learn and the nature of the relationships between their peers and other adults. Whether you work in a purpose-built or adapted early years setting, or in your own home, the choices you make, including who you employ and their attitudes and beliefs, will reveal both the priorities of the setting and the underlying values of those in it.

As children continue to develop, even more is happening in the brain, and they are becoming more individual as the months pass, exploring their place and their growing personalities. As children move through early years settings, they should, if they have been at the setting since they were babies, already be familiar with the routines and expectations of the setting and have some understanding of the boundaries that are in place. By the time they reach their third birthday, unless there are concerns surrounding their speech and language development, children should be able to form short sentences spontaneously to communicate with those around them. At this stage, language development is still rapid, and they have a better understanding of body language, vocabulary and how to interact, in varying degrees, with their peers and adults. Many relationships within the setting may already have been formed; however, for those moving rooms and joining the setting at 3 or 4, the time to adjust to their new surroundings and the people who work with them needs to be carefully considered.

The Mosaic approach: listening to children

Clark and Moss (2005) developed the Mosaic approach (2005:5) as a way of listening to children that 'acknowledges children and adults as co-constructors of meaning' (Clark & Moss, 2011:1). It places children as 'experts in their own lives' (2005:6) and supports the suggestion that children have a 'unique perspective . . . about their own lives' (Clark & Moss, 2005:6). This is certainly the case for pre-school children, and the project, whilst originally carried out with 3- and 4-year-olds, has now been adapted for those under 2 and children who are non-verbal or who have English as an additional language. Children seem to be a never-ending font of knowledge, questioning everything and, if they are able, telling anyone who will listen about their lives and important events. It has been argued that 'listening to young children is an integral part of understanding what they are feeling and experiencing' (Pascal & Bertram, 2009:254) and forms the basis for all our interactions with them.

It is crucial in our relationships with children and our daily interactions with them that we first learn to listen. Whilst many practitioners understand this to mean only to those who can communicate verbally; in fact, we now know that communication is much more than just what a child expresses verbally. Many settings will readily talk about how the voice of the child is respected and listened to in their provision, but 'listening to young children, including pre-verbal children, needs to be a process which is open to the many creative ways young children use to express their views and experiences' (Clark & Moss, 2011:7).

When that child walks through the door, when ANY child walks through the door, let your eyes light up at the sight of them. Let that child, in that moment, know that they are loved and valued. Connection is the key to almost any behaviour. When a child is having a tantrum – connection. When a child is crying at drop off – connection. When a child is having trouble controlling their body or their emotions – connection.

Communication

The way we speak to children can have an impact on the way they view themselves and is crucial when looking at the relationships we form with them. As children turn 2 and 3, their vocabulary is growing rapidly, but this can only be the case if we provide children with a language-rich environment and give them access to a range of books, props, literacy-based invitations to explore and, most importantly, use our own and their experiences to make it all relevant. We know children learn best when they are motivated and highly engaged, and the only way this can be achieved is by tuning in to their fascinations and the things that interest them.

The language we use, of course, has to be adapted depending on the age of the child, and it is well known that speaking to babies in a motherese style can support attachment and social skills in infancy; however, continuing to use made-up words and baby talk beyond the baby stage can have detrimental effects on language development, something which we are seeing in the aftermath of the coronavirus pandemic. Young children need to know they are respected; it stands to reason then that, as early years educators, we should speak to them like they are human beings having thoughts and developing feelings of their own. We cannot expect children to learn language if we are not modelling what it should sound like and treating them as though they don't understand mature vocabulary.

Many parents don't see the harm in calling a train a 'choo choo', a bottle a 'bot bot' or their child 'baba', but as a child reaches 3 or 4, children are more than capable of understanding what they are and saying the words, and if you want the children you work with to use language effectively, we need to be modelling how it should sound by using real words and real sentences. It is vital that we use our knowledge to educate parents, and whilst it is not our place to tell them how to bring up their children, we can offer advice and support and ensure they have all the information regarding the impact their actions can have in the long term. Children will come up with their own words and phrases as they learn language, and that is a completely normal stage in the acquisition of language, but it is our role as respectful educators to show children the right way, repeating their attempts and extending them, ensuring that we use every opportunity to develop their language skills and vocabulary. There is a reason that communication and language is one of the prime areas of the early years foundation stage, and put simply, it is because without it, there is very little progress within the other areas. Early relationships are formed with babies before they can speak, but as children get older, the way they extend and build on those relationships is through language.

Children with speech and language delays provide evidence for us that although many are still social and show communicative intent, without the skills required to join in with others and to extend play with their peers, they remain largely on the periphery of what social communication can do for them in the early years.

The attitudes of staff towards children and what they are capable of can also have a huge impact on communication with young children. We know that children from around the age of 2 begin to exert their autonomy and their developing sense of self. Keeping sentences short and to the point when working with young children will support their ability to understand what it is we want from them whilst avoiding using nonsense words or baby talk, as we have seen this can have a detrimental effect on children's development of language. However, something even worse can occur when we continue to use this type of language with children of 3 or 4 years old. Children are quick learners, and we know that they will tend to copy those around them; however, when practitioners and parents continue to treat pre-school children as though they are infants or toddlers, their sense of self begins to suffer. Children of around 3 years old, although they may not be able to express themselves to the extent of an older child, have been immersed in language learning since before they were born, listening to sounds in the womb and being spoken to from birth. They deserve much more credit than many give them, and continuing to speak down to them as though they lack understanding inevitably has a lasting impact on their self-esteem, confidence and ability to develop those vital skills of resilience and perseverance.

The terrible twos

Children's perception of the way they are viewed by others can also give rise to frustration and anger, often resulting in what many parents call the terrible twos. Having worked in early years for the best part of eighteen years, it is a term I dislike greatly, and I don't think I am alone in this. These stereotypical labels are extremely unhelpful in understanding and, therefore, unpicking what the child is trying to communicate. For early years practitioners with knowledge of children's developmental changes, we know that the brain is going through some major changes as children try and find their place. For many, they still haven't worked out how to effectively communicate their needs, and even if they have, sometimes the emotions are so overwhelming that with the best will in the world, what results is a screaming, shouting, crying shell of a child

trying to tell us something. The difficulty in this situation is what to do about it, and it is here that the attitudes of the staff and what they understand about the children in their care really matter. For this, we need to change our perspective.

There will no doubt be some practitioners reading this who believe in the terrible twos, who have used it to justify behaviours to parents at handover or who have nodded when parents suggest that their child has hit the terrible twos. If this sounds like you, I'm glad you're here. It has always been my hope that this book will facilitate reflection and start an open dialogue within settings to evaluate why they do what they do and the values they hold. If you have ever heard a parent refer to their child as going through the terrible twos, it is important that, using our knowledge, we support parents to challenge their thinking and reframe their ideas around what may be happening for their child at this important stage. It is important to note that it is just that, a stage. An important, albeit frustrating, one for parents and practitioners alike, but one that every child must go through. We often find that if a child doesn't go through this phase of transition and rapid brain development any time from their second birthday up to the time they turn 3, you can almost guarantee they will experience increased frustrations in their pre-school years as they have not developed the strategies they need.

It can sometimes be obvious what the matter might be – if a child has taken the toy they were playing with, if they are hurt or if they are trying to put a shoe on and it doesn't fit. These are usually all quick fixes with some mindful observation, contextual clues and an offer of help if they would like it; these things can be solved, and the child calms quickly, resuming their play. What happens, though, when it isn't a quick fix, when there aren't any clues as to what happened or when a child is simply distressed because they wanted something that wasn't available or something beyond your control (like wanting Mummy or a chocolate biscuit for snack). This is where it is even more important to remain calm and have a consistent response at the ready that everyone understands. For many parents and practitioners, the need to appease or solve everything for a child can be overwhelming, especially if a child is upset and appears inconsolable, but often, this is not helpful and can be detrimental to the child and their view of themselves. These inconsistencies in approach lead to confusion for the child who will no longer understand what is expected and, therefore, cannot build new neural connections that will build the foundations for socially acceptable behaviour later on.

The way we communicate with a child who is upset will depend upon the cause and whether our intervention can in fact make it better. It is important that any strategy we have in place has the child at the centre, something which can be more difficult to manage in larger settings or those belonging to a chain who have predetermined policies and ideas about how behaviour should be managed. The difficulty here is that often, a one-size-fits-all approach is used. What works for one child will almost certainly not work for them all; after all, we know that children are all different and their level of maturity and development has different rates. How then can we use one approach for all situations?

The most effective way for settings to manage behaviour is to have agreed values and reflect on what they want to promote within their setting, as well as an understanding of how they approach consequences with young children. This is much easier to try and achieve than simply prescribing to one method and hoping that it works for everyone, which in my experience is rarely

the case. Each situation needs to be dealt with on an individual basis, considering what the practitioners know about the child and 'practice is more effective if viewed as an ongoing approach and one that includes team members and parents sharing their views on what discipline, boundaries or managing behaviour means to them' (Manning-Morton & Thorp, 2015:79). It is no good trying to explain in detail another child's perspective when the child you're talking to is crying and overwhelmed with emotions that they can't understand. Knowledge of child development is crucial here, as without it, it is highly likely that the child's needs are not going to be met and the cycle of unrealistic expectations and failed behaviour management strategies will continue. One of the most effective ways to tackle this is by using the key person approach to your advantage, ensuring children know who they can rely on for support in times of emotional distress.

The key person approach

The setting I manage is a day nursery catering for over sixty children every day, and we have largely open-plan rooms for four overlapping age groups. The beauty of working with children and transitioning them based on their development and not always on their birthday means that staff can form relationships that last anywhere from 12 months to 2 years and have an in-depth understanding of exactly what a child needs at a given time based on where they are now, not where we would like them to be as a condition of moving into the next room or to the next stage in a tick list. The key person approach ensures that all children have not only a named practitioner who is responsible for their day-to-day care and development but someone who they can build a strong, trusting relationship with and come to rely upon when they need support or encouragement. It is usually this person who in turn forges a relationship with the family that will then be carried into the other rooms within the setting.

Following the work of Bowlby and Ainsworth, attachment theory plays a huge role in why the key person approach was written into the early years foundation stage framework in 2008. We know how important it is for children to feel safe and secure in their environment in order to thrive, and having a familiar adult who advocates for your needs is just one of the ways we can encourage and support children to feel welcomed and valued in our settings. Part of the key person role includes observing children. This is perhaps the most important element of the role. This will in turn give an accurate assessment of what children are capable of, when they truly need help and what their emotional triggers are; by knowing this, you will be able to facilitate what they need. Staff at Nina's Nursery High Lane use the key person approach to ensure they form strong bonds with each child and their family in order for children to thrive.

It is also vital that a child's key person advocates for them if they are unable to do it for themselves. This revisits the idea that staff must have strong relationships with parents if they are to support them through a children's formative years. For pre-school children who start pre-school at 3, we must be even more patient as they may lack knowledge and understanding of behavioural expectations, especially if they come from a home of inconsistent boundaries, resulting in confusion and sometimes frustrated, angry outbursts. It is then the role of the key person, not only to ensure that child feels safe and welcomed into the setting but to show them, through modelling and attentive observation, how to be part of a social group that they are unfamiliar with. They must also work with parents to share effective ways to reduce triggers and provide consistent behaviour strategies; however, it is worth noting that this can only be done where the parent wants support. Unfortunately, it can be the case that parents are unaware of their child's difficulties in social situations as they do not arise at home and, subsequently, do not work in partnership with the setting. In these instances, we can hope for warm, consistent, nurturing relationships with staff and educating parents that 'discipline, guiding children's behaviour or setting limits are all concerned with helping children learn how to take care of themselves, other people and the world around them' (Greenman & Stonehouse, 1996:138).

Interaction

> promoting creativity . . . is to do with how we maximise our use of the environment we
> find ourselves in and draw out the most from our interactions with the children.
>
> (Duffy, 2006:181)

Interaction with adults is vital if children are to learn how to connect with others. They will
have a certain number of interactions with their peers, but for the most part, especially in the
case of toddlers, if their language skills are still developing, it is the adults they work with who
provide a model of language and social engagement. This is why it is so important that children
are respected as equal in these interactions and are given the opportunity to engage (or not).
Giving a child choice has a huge impact on their ability to understand themselves as individuals.
Too often, life happens *to* young children rather than with them, and by offering choices and
giving them the opportunity to make their own decisions, whilst not overwhelming them, we
are sending them the message that they are important.

Drawing on the work of theorists such as Bronfenbrenner, who revised his own theory
The Ecology of Human Development several times over the years, we know that all those who
interact with children and the environments in which they do so have an impact on a child's
overall development to varying degrees. In his revised theory, he discusses the importance of
interactions that happen between the child and their surroundings and argues that 'human development takes place through the processes of progressively more complex reciprocal interaction
between an active, evolving biopsychological human organism and the persons, objects and
symbols in the immediate external environment' (Bronfenbrenner, 1995:620). It is true that
children are affected by their experiences, their interactions with others and the environments
that they encounter, but how much of what we are and what we will become is innate, and

whether there are a set of 'innate, hierarchical, human needs and motivations' (Abulof, 2017:1) is still being debated.

What is important here is to remember that children can be deeply affected by the environment and their interactions with the world around them, so it is vital that we get it right. This includes not interfering and can be something that many early years practitioners find extremely difficult. Again, with almost everything, an understanding of child development is vital here. Practitioners need to be able to understand not only where the child is developmentally but the extent to which any interaction can support and encourage further learning or whether it may hinder the child's natural ability to follow their own interests. Even when children are playing alone, this doesn't automatically mean that they need engagement from staff members or encouragement to find a friend, as can be a common phrase in early years. There is a fine line between interacting and interfering, something that Julie Fisher talks about in her book *Interacting or Interferring?*. Often, what is just as important as the interaction itself is stepping back and observing the child and what may be going on in each moment. Regardless of the age of the child, if they are happy in their play whether alone or with friends, it is the skilled practitioner who can stand back and observe.

For many who are not used to this way of working, it can seem like they aren't doing very much, and some can worry that if a member of management sees them, it will look like they aren't doing anything at all. I am not suggesting that if all the children are engaged that practitioners use the opportunity to catch up with their colleagues about their weekend plans; it should instead be a chance to reflect, watch and decide whether you can add to the child's experience or learning, much as is the case with in the moment planning. Simply sitting near to a child is enough for them to make eye contact or a request. For children who have the ability to communicate, they will often ask practitioners and invite them into their play. For younger children, specifically those between 2 and 3 who may be in the early stages of language acquisition or those who speak English as an additional language and may not have the ability to form full sentences, it is up to practitioners to look for non-verbal cues that children need support.

Expectations

The very early theories of Emmi Pikler provide thought-provoking insights into the way we expect young children to behave. She suggests that adults are responsible for hindering 'children's independence and feeling of competence . . . under the pretext of "helping" they deprive a child of the possibility of taking the initiative, of trying things out and bringing them to a finish'. Moreover, she adds that this 'takes away the feeling of effectiveness, as does the sort of traditional helping in which an adult does something with or to the child, as though s/he were an object' (Pikler, 1979). This is why practitioners need to think carefully before interrupting what could be deep-level learning and play. Skilled practitioners use their knowledge of the children they work with to decide whether or not an interaction is needed.

As we have already explored, it is often much easier for an adult to do something for the child when they look as though they are struggling, but it is this struggle that provides the most learning. Children need to be allowed time to struggle, and whilst I am not suggesting we leave them distressed for prolonged periods, neither is it helpful to solve all their problems, dress them and appease them at the detriment of others. Children learn cooperation, patience, resilience and perseverance through the opportunity to experience it, and it is our duty to ensure we give them enough chances to do so.

It has been said that 'Piaget's views led him to undervalue the role of the adult' (Duffy, 2006:119). Piaget and his theory of cognitive development rely heavily on the idea that children go through different stages at different ages but that they must pass through all of them; because of this, Duffy suggests that 'children are not presented with challenging experiences because they are not deemed ready to understand them' (2006:119). This is vital when we consider what we expect of young children and why it is important that as early years practitioners; we have high expectations of the children we work with to ensure they are challenging their thinking and developing the skills they need to develop creatively.

Alongside the idea of expectations is the notion of learned helplessness. This is a relatively new term that describes children who are more than capable of carrying out tasks for themselves but don't, often as a result of the adults in their lives not allowing them to do things for themselves. Some of these behaviours are already established by the time a child reaches the age of 2, and the older a child is, the harder it is to support and encourage them out of helplessness; even if they are more than capable of doing something, they will lack the self-esteem, confidence and positive attitude to carry it out. Children develop independence and a strong sense of self from the age of around 18 months. The danger of learned helplessness is that if parents and those adults working with children don't recognise this growth and potentially continue taking steps to hinder it, such as being fed, dressed, escorted or carried from place to place when they are more than capable of doing it for themselves, they continue to have a learned dependency on others which can be extremely detrimental to their later childhood years.

What is abundantly clear is the relationship between adult and children during the years following their second birthday mean just as much as those first bonds created in infancy. As children develop and push boundaries and discover their limits, it is the role of the adults in early years to be the calm in their storm. Children are only doing what they are programmed for, and that is to find out where they fit in the world and what power they have. The only way to do this is to question, through pushing boundaries, 'what happens if I do this? What will you do if this happens?'. Children need us to calmly and firmly answer their questions, yes; the response may change from time to time, as we have explained, we cannot and should not try to make them happy all the time, but they will learn that we will lead and guide them in a way that supports their overall development. They need that from us. Children of all ages need connections with those around them, and building and maintaining strong relationships with children and their families will enable them to develop their understanding of the social world and will form the foundations of deeper-level learning and creative thinking.

6 Developing an environment for creativity

The spaces and environments we create for children are important when looking at the types of behaviour and skills we are trying to encourage. Prescriptive activities, rigid routines and environments devoid of children's true interests and fascinations are not conducive to developing a sense of freedom and creativity for young children, especially those with developing skills. In this chapter, we will explore some of the important elements of an environment that promotes free creative thinking and the distinct differences between what we provide for younger children, and what is needed to create a space conducive to creativity for older children, who are often physically more capable and ready for more challenges.

It is impossible to apply the same principles to all age groups, regardless of whether you work in a large day nursery, home setting or provision that offers sessional care. Whilst we can carry the same values and ethos throughout the setting, we cannot offer the same opportunities. Babies and younger children up to the age of 2 need a very different environment from that of a confident, physically able 3- or 4-year-old. We can agree that they both need space to move, to play, to

DOI: 10.4324/9781003271710-8

challenge their skills and thinking, and a place to feel calm, reflect and share a story with an adult should they choose, but what these spaces look like will differ greatly. For babies, challenging their physicality may mean providing opportunities to play at different heights, to encourage cruising and standing independently and early climbing or playing on ramps. When we consider older children, the idea of physical challenge means climbing, often at height, introducing swings and tyres and lots of opportunity to develop growing skills such as balancing or jumping appropriately. This is something that Bright Stars Nursery in Sunderland have worked hard to incorporate in their outdoor environment, ensuring that children have the opportunity to develop a range of skills.

Those in home-based settings have the difficult task of thinking about and providing appropriate challenge for a range of age groups, often within the same space, whilst those in large day nurseries benefit from rooms designed with a particular age group and their needs in mind. No matter what type of provision you have, this chapter aims to provide the opportunity to think about what is important for children when designing place spaces for them and how we can continue to promote creativity through the environment.

Emotional environment

The environment we create for children is so important in terms of development and the experiences they have available to them. It is vital that we remember, though, that without a high-quality emotional environment, children will not thrive. The emotional environment we create for children supports their overall wellbeing and sense of belonging. We know as adults the difference we feel when we are comfortable and have people and things around us that matter to us. The same can be said for those in early years settings, and the physical environment we design goes hand in hand with the emotional environment that we create by showing children they are valued and listened to and that, as adults, we respect their choices and acknowledge their needs at any given time. For a child to thrive, they need to feel safe and loved and part of a larger community to which they belong. For 2- and 3-year-olds, this is often as simple as ensuring that all the children have their own coat peg, they have a name or photograph and they know where to hang their things. Early self-registration could be as simple as asking children to find their photo-graph and using velcro to add it to a board, showing who is playing today. For pre-school-age children who may be beginning to recognise their name, self-registration is a great way to embed the meaning in print and support name recognition; children not yet able would benefit from a photograph alongside their name as they begin to connect the meaning. By having somewhere to hang their things every day, children begin to develop a sense that they belong.

A family wall, a 'special treasures' display table, photos, and keepsakes from each family's culture available, words and quotes displayed in the child's home language. All of these contribute to that wonderful feeling of 'belonging' to the space.

(Carlene Cox-Newton)

How we greet children and families also goes a long way to developing a high-quality emo-tional environment, leaving stressors behind and greeting children with a friendly face and a smile tells them straight away that they are wanted and you are happy to see them. If practitioners fail to see the importance of the emotional environment, even with older children, they can become withdrawn, quiet and not willing to engage in a range of activities.

Transitional times

Something that goes hand in hand with the emotional environment that is created for young children are transitional times throughout the day and how these are managed by the adults in the room. The most important of them all is when children come into the setting each morning. If this is not managed sensitively, it can set the child up for an emotionally diffi-cult day. The idea of transitional objects, first put forward by Winnicott (2005), is important when we consider the emotional environment we create for children. Many children will attend settings with an object, usually a soft toy that they use for comfort and as a way to bridge the gap between what they need and subsequently get. For children starting nur-sery or pre-school for the first time, the sense of anxiety they feel may be high, depending on their past experiences. Many use comforters, toys or sometimes other objects to bridge the separation they feel. Think of it as an object that connects them to their home and family. A comforter often smells of home or even a parent which, when faced with separ-ation from those things, can support the child and allow them to feel close to them when they are not there. You can see then how expecting a child to hand over their comforter, whether it's a blanket, cuddly toy or other object, is going to end in distress and anxiety for the child. I am not saying that we should allow children to walk around with them all day, especially at 3 and 4, but there should be strategies in place to allow the child to settle in, thus rendering the comforter unnecessary. Families should be encouraged to bring in photographs of important people and most settings now have parents complete an all-about-me-style booklet before starting. This allows practitioners an insight into the child and provides the child with tangible items that can be shared with a practitioner in times of need.

Some transitional moments, such as moving to mealtimes or rest or those that involve chil-dren getting ready to go home, can often feel like military operations. Moving children from one activity to another through a process of doing things to and for children rather than with them can create the feeling that the children are not at the centre of the routine and staff are simply trying to get things done. As children develop their independence, practitioners have a respon-sibility to ensure that they are given as many opportunities as possible and support them with emerging skills. Too often, practitioners, in a hurry to get things done, miss vital chances for the children they work with to exercise their autonomy, do things for themselves or communicate effectively in order to get what they need. Missing these opportunities has a detrimental effect on the development of these important skills. Children very quickly learn that staff will do things for them if they protest long enough.

Physical space

The experiences on offer to children are only a part of what it is like to be a child at your provision. The adults that support them make up another part, but it is in fact the phys-ical space we have for children and what we choose to fill it with that creates the founda-tion for what happens each day. A well-planned and designed area for children filled with resources that give them the opportunity to engage in a wide range of activities is the most effective way of ensuring children are developing to their full potential. It doesn't matter whether you have a large purpose-built setting, a home-based provision or an outdoor nur-sery. The space you have available will guide how you arrange it, the furniture you use and potential storage options, especially if you are looking for something space-saving. As with most things in early years, seeing it from a child's perspective is the most effective way of reflecting and making any changes. It is important to consider schematic play patterns and ensure you have a balance of open plan areas that provide children with the opportunity for large-scale play and space to move freely but also smaller areas for those children who like to feel enclosed and cosy, and have a space to relax and sleep if they need to. This is something the team at Scallywags Nursery have considered when designing their spaces for young children.

The layout of the play space we have will depend greatly on what we have available to us, and we must acknowledge our limits if we are to overcome them. If there is not a large space available, having an indoor climbing frame, for example, may not be possible; provision for climbing can be moved outside, or frames that mount to walls and can be folded flat are a great way to save space. As practitioners, whether we think so or not, we are quite creative in the way we approach and solve problems. This can be used to your advantage when deciding how to set up a room for children. Toddlers require lots of open space but also places to be creative, take part in imaginative play, share a story with a friend or spend time building. As children begin to push boundaries, though, it is important we do not set them up to fail, and we can do this by thinking carefully about the environment we have. If we want to encourage walking indoors and not running, having large runways through rooms invites children to do just that. Think back to the idea of a yes space for children where we try, not to remove boundaries but to make it possible for children to follow them. By breaking up runways, children will be less likely to run indoors. The same can be said about jumping on furniture or throwing. At 2 years old, these are normal behaviours as children find out what they can and can't do within the context of an early years setting. We can again use our environment to our advantage here. By making sure there is provision for children's interests, they will be less likely to engage in unwanted behaviours.

Colour

Without realising it, we spend more time in our workplace than we do at home. The same can be said for some children. Whilst it is the case that some children access only a few hours a week, others spend up to fifty hours in early years provision. It is important then that we reflect on the environment and ensure we are doing everything we can to give children the best experience, and this includes thinking about the décor and colour palettes we use in young children's play spaces. As adults, we are drawn to certain colour schemes, we decorate our homes with them, and for the most part, ensuring our homes are clutter-free and calming means we can relax at the end of a busy day. There are not many of us who would choose red walls for our living rooms or florescent colours in our bedrooms. This is because we know the effect that colour can have on our mood.

Historically, early years settings were visually stimulating. Boxes of brightly colours plastic toys, bricks and character paraphernalia were out, tipped on tables for the children to play with or stored in brightly coloured cupboards. The result is children who are unable to stay focussed, think creatively or stay engaged from prolonged periods of time. Times are changing, and leaders of early years are beginning to reflect on the environment and the effect that this overstimulation is having on children. Calming tones close to those in nature are being favoured by many and keep overstimulation to a minimum. Olive green, pale blues and purples are also known to create a feeling of relaxation. Another reason settings are choosing to tone down their environments, as well as reducing sensory stimulation, is to ensure that what they do have in the environment and the colours they use are purposeful and have meaning. The children are the most important thing in any environment, after all; it is them that inhabit it. Artwork and photographs are much more likely to be seen on plain, neutral backgrounds than patterns, meaning children feel a sense of value and belonging, and they see their work, and it doesn't get lost in the garish surroundings.

Lighting

Artificial and bright lights can be overstimulating for lots of children; if you have access to natural light, this should be utilised as much as possible by opening blinds or curtains and ensuring it can cascade through the room. This will also enable you to consider switching off the harsh artificial lights. If you are not lucky enough to benefit from a purpose-built setting and, therefore, have limited natural light, as is the case in the pre-school room of my setting, it is vital that you reflect on what you can do to ensure children have time away from potentially harmful fluorescent or strip lighting.

This is something that Bright Stars nursery do particularly well. Staff reflect on their environment regularly to make sure it meets the needs of the children. They pay close attention to the way it feels for a child in their setting and create a feeling of warmth throughout.

Adding fairy lights to the environment and lamps to smaller, cosy spaces means that at least for some of the day, strip lighting can be switched off and children can feel a sense of warmth from warm white light. Whilst natural lighting is best, this is not always possible, and adjustments must be made to ensure children are not overstimulated or distracted by harsh light sources.

Sound

> There is often a cacophony of sounds in an early years setting: children chatter and laughter, adults, occasional recorded background music and even the resources in the setting all have an impact and can sometimes interfere with the harmony of the environment.
>
> (Johnson & Watts, 2019:65)

Children can be extremely sensitive to the sounds around them; background noise is a fact of life; the hustle and bustle of play spaces and what will eventually be a classroom environment can often be very loud. Even at home, there is usually constant noise from televisions and devices, and even in the car, conversation has been replaced and parents listen to the radio. Children, by the time they arrive in settings, have already listened to more auditory input that most of us listen to all day. Perhaps then we can start to see why there is a decrease in children's ability to stay focussed and listen to instructions, and why they become easily distracted.

There will always be some level of noise in a busy toddler room or pre-school, possibly even more so for childminders who have a range of ages all playing together, but it should never be so loud that children cannot think. The chattering of children whilst they play is music to anyone who works in early years. What children don't need is unnecessary music from a CD player in the corner of the room, drowning out instructions and natural sound sources. Open a window and let the birds sing, let children hear traffic and then talk to their friends about it. Often, children will talk about what they hear when it is natural occurring, a digger working on a nearby yard, a motorbike or the birds. Rarely have I heard a child say, 'I loved the choice of CD music today'.

A yes space

We have already looked briefly at the idea of a yes space within the environment, but what about how to create one? A yes space for children promotes individual ideas and expression and allows children to follow their interests without the interference of others. In terms of the emotional environment, a yes space is a place where we refrain from negative language and reframe our thinking to allow children the opportunity to do things their way. This can include the way we think about our continuous provision.

Continuous provision refers to those resources and spaces that remain constant in the environment. Water, sand, dough, art, blocks and other staples of the early years environment. In order for our environment to support a yes space, we must reflect on what we provide for the children and what resources they have access to within it. In his book *Can I go and play now?*, Gregg

Bottrill makes some suggestions as to how we can ensure we are getting our environment right for children and allowing them to explore their own ideas and not ours. He writes this:

> If I like playing in the water and want to explore its journey down ramps or through pipes but the adult has meticulously set up a zone with dinosaurs and a selection of rocks and pebbles with a plastic island in the middle all bedecked with foam numbers, can I as a child explore that zone as I wish? Is the adult not interpreting the space even before I have arrived with my childish imagination and dreams?

This is an extremely valid point and returns to the idea of adults, often thinking if they don't set up or provide interesting invitations for the children that they are not doing anything. This is far from the truth. It is a much better use of time to ensure that you have identified areas that the children enjoy spending their time and provide as many different opportunities as possible for the children within them. This will give children the freedom to choose what to do with the space and the materials provided rather than feel they can only have what has been put out for them.

Lindsay Moore, founder of Butterflies of Britain Nature Education programme, runs a nature play centre in Suffolk. She observed children's interest in gluing their hands and started to think about ways she could incorporate this into her continuous provision.

> I had a box of broken resources which I had kept for loose parts and the magic just happened. Using a pallet and tubs and pump bottles of glue the children just started using the broken and found resources to stick to the pallet. From there I asked parents to donate treasures, bottle lids etc. Now we have a working project, the table of broken and lost treasure. Children bring in so many things for it and it's wonderful to see.

This is not to say that provocations based on the children's fascinations cannot be set up, and Lindsay's treasure table is a great example of why they absolutely should, but practitioners must remain mindful of what they set up and why. Consider how you can give children the opportunity to explore freely without providing a dinosaur world or rock pool already set up. If children have everything they need in their environment, observant adults can see the play unfold and offer ideas and suggestions. The child may end up with an elaborate dinosaur world complete with volcano and forests, but there will be deeper-level learning and engagement if they were supported in setting it up themselves rather than adult assuming that is what they wanted to play with.

Of course, like with every aspect of the environment, it must support the children it serves. Younger children who may lack the communicative ability to share their thoughts and ideas verbally may respond well to a thoughtful small-world setup to extend their play. Keeping the children at the heart of what you do will ensure that you are providing the chance for children to think for themselves and engage with activities that inspire them.

Resources or themed spaces?

When we consider the layout of a room or area for young children, we often think about the resources that we want to use and how we can display them. For those with home-based settings, this can pose a challenge as the spaces they have available are often smaller than that of nurseries or pre-schools, so they have to be mindful of using too much furniture and think creatively about their choice of storage solutions. Childminders also have a unique perspective when it comes to creating a home from home environment as, unlike nurseries, they are exactly that. Amanda Calloway, from CheekyRascalz Childminding, understands that children need to be cared for in well-thought-out environments in order to thrive.

> Giving children ample opportunity for active learning, developing their own critical thinking skills and instilling a love of nature. I aim to be a mindful practitioner, always reflecting and questioning my practice to make it the best possible environment for the children.

Many day nurseries will theme areas and continuous provision. It is common to see resources organised so that similar objectives or resources are together for children to be able extend their ideas and have everything they need to do so close by.

Dominique Adema reflects on the role play opportunities she provides and ensures that there are lots of authentic resources within easy reach so children can fully explore their own narratives.

There are no hard and fast rules about setting up spaces for young children; it will depend entirely on the cohort you have and their needs. It is often the case that as children move through rooms, the environment needs to be reflected on and changes made to meet the needs of the current children. It is easy to follow pages on social media and try to recreate such play spaces and areas of provision, but practitioners then wonder why they are not seeing the same level of engagement from their children. The reason is simple. Children need spaces that are designed with them in mind.

Block play

Areas for block play and large-scale construction are often close by, as this type of play complement each other, and children will often extend their ideas using the resources available to them. Block play should be set up in an area that is free from other distractions and out of traffic areas, allowing children the opportunity to focus, and there should be enough blocks that both large- and small-scale structures can be built without running out. The space for block play is critical since pre-schoolers tend to do more constructive play where larger, complex structures are made with larger-sized blocks and many children working together. It is essential the block space is large enough to accommodate this type of play. Accessories such as people, animals and transportation vehicles should also be available to expand play and give children the chance to introduce a narrative.

The Early Childhood Environment Rating Scale – Revised Edition recommends block play or construction areas should be big enough to allow at least three children to build sizable structures, and the blocks should be stored in low open shelves to allow children to access them independently.

Art areas

Children need to have a wide range of art materials as their skills develop, and the way they use them will begin to change as they explore further what they can do and as their ideas develop. Whilst many 2-year-olds love to body paint, covering their arms and all available skin in all the colours of the rainbow, most 3- and 4-year-olds will have left this stage behind, opting for other ways to express themselves. Practitioners need to remember to keep the child at the centre of art-making, respecting where they are and what they can do rather than trying to impose their ideas and conveyor craft plans on young children. Only by doing this will children know and trust that they have the freedom to create what and how they choose.

However, practitioners can strike a balance when working with pre-school children between freedom of choice and adult-guided invitations. Whilst I strongly believe that for the most part, children should be given every opportunity to exercise their autonomy, there are occasions where their endeavours should be closely supervised and guided by adults. I understand this will depend on how your setting plans for young children, if at all, and the way in which sessions are run and organised as explained in Chapter 3; however, to plan an environment that supports children's creativity and independent thinking, there may be times when we, as adults, can add value to their ideas by introducing to them new concepts, materials or ways of doing things.

In our pre-school play space, we have some art resources organised according to the level of supervision or guidance a material might need. Higher risk resources are kept on a slightly higher shelf but still within sight of the children; that way, they can ask for it if they'd like. We also store a variety of materials for projects, such as Modroc, wire and plaster of Paris; these are, like the other resources, on the shelves so the children can see them and ask for them if they'd like to use them. Many settings do not allow children to use scissors, so therefore, store them out of reach. Some choose to stay within the confines of ready-mixed paint and PVA. It is crucial that you understand the needs of your children and where they are developmentally before deciding what resources should be readily available and those that need to be stored differently. It is not my intention to advocate for a particular way of doing things, simply to provide a platform for practitioners to consider their options.

Woodworking and tinkering

Woodworking with young children has a multitude of benefits. From early problem-solving, mark-making and safe handling of tools to potentially elaborate projects, experiencing with drills and saws and creating structures with the support of a trusted adult. Children also develop their communication and language, increase their vocabulary, and practise their fine motor control as well as a range of critical thinking skills, such as designing, making decisions about how to do things, carrying out their ideas and evaluating their projects. 'Children are drawn in as they explore possibilities, rise to challenges and find solutions' (Moorhouse, 2018:4).

Many leaders in early years shy away from woodwork as part of their curriculum due to the perceived risks and health and safety concerns, but as Nina's Nursery High Lane know, the benefits of working with tools far outweigh the potential risks, and with close supervision and modelling, children thrive.

Woodwork promotes creativity and critical thinking, and we, therefore, need to reflect on the provision we have and find ways to overcome our own preconceived ideas about what might happen and instead start to think about the positive impact woodworking with children can have. If you are unsure of where to start, consider evaluating your current provision for working with tools, constructing and developing collaborative, creative thinking. For young children who are still developing, playing with wooden loose parts, gluing wooden objects together, hammering and doing activities such as Hapa Zome using child-sized hammers are all introductions to woodwork and working with tools, that will be utilised later when they have further developed some level of controlled movement and listening skills.

At Wally's, we are lucky to have a woodworking and tinkering shed in pre-school. With space for two children to work side by side, we have a workbench, tools, a range of sizes and shapes of wooden offcuts, dowels, and other pieces of wood as well as nuts and bolts, screws and even a computer that the children have unscrewed and begun to investigate. Tinkering and working with their hands are great ways for children to try out new ideas and see what they can create. Children can combine pieces using woodworking techniques, or for those who would prefer, PVA and glue guns work just as well in order to connect two pieces together.

Baking

Cooking with children is something that is crucial in supporting their development in many areas. Toddlers are more than capable of listening for short periods, particularly when activities interest them, and I am yet to meet a toddler who doesn't love to bake. This is an example of a guided activity with 2-year-olds, and as they become more confident and their skills develop, they can begin to manage some risks and cook independently of adults. There are some great easy-to-make recipes for young children, and there is often so much more to it than simply making something nice to eat. Children develop early mathematical concepts of weighing and measuring, exploring heavy and light, and learning about food in a hands-on way. Cooking with children is also known to support those children with food aversions or special educational needs as they make contact with a range of foodstuff and various tastes and textures, and have increased exposure to food which often results in increased confidence to try new foods.

Provision for cooking is often something that practitioners shy away from, and many settings don't cook with their children at all. This could be because of health and safety concerns, potential allergens or simply lack of experience and equipment. It is easy to get started with the basics of cooking with children, even if you don't have access to a kitchen. Children enjoy weighing ingredients and mixing to make potions and pies, usually outdoors in mud kitchens. This can easily be transferred to the context of cooking, even if children are given flour and water. They will begin to use early mathematical thinking to combine what is available and more than likely proudly present what they have made. You could experiment with children making their own play dough if baking is not accessible, something which is simple to do and brings a similar satisfaction to cooking.

If you do have access to an oven or microwave, there are lots of simple recipes that lend themselves to toddlers and pre-school children that they can begin to cook independently. Children receive language-rich experiences through cooking with adults and learn to name different kitchen utensils and ways to cook. Pre-school children who can retain a little more information can begin to memorise simple recipes, collaborate with others and learn key concepts as well as basic safety measures and hand hygiene. A great addition to any pre-school that does facilitate cooking is an induction hob. These are simple and safe to use and can be placed on tabletops for children to make a variety of recipes, some of which I will share in Part 2. It goes without saying that if you are cooking with young children, remember to be vigilant with hand-washing routines and aware of any children in the group with allergies.

Reflective practice

Your environment is, as Langston and Abbott (2004:70) suggest, 'more than simply the planned space in the setting; it is everything that is encountered from the point of entry to the setting to the point of departure'. Whatever space you have available, there are likely to be constraints of space, time and often money but children still need an environment where they have opportunities to explore the world through all their senses in order to develop. Nicholson (2005:50) sees the physical building as a 'second skin' where children are at the centre of what is happening, and communication and collaboration takes place easily. Laevers (2005:22) suggests that the 'richness' of the environment can be tested through two principles, those of diversity (how broad is the horizon of possible experiences?) and depth (how much is there to be discovered?). He highlights the adult's role in setting up an environment where such exploration can happen. Consider, in relation to your early years setting, the question he poses: 'Is the reality brought into the setting complex enough or is it processed by the adult up to the point where the joy of discovery, adventure and serendipity altogether is banned from the daily life of children?' (Laevers, 2005:22).

At Busy Bunnies, children access open-ended resources independently to ensure they have a range of opportunities to develop their creativity.

> We keep our resources open-ended so the only limit on what they can be is the child's imagination. Opportunities to create art, bake, cook, engineer, grow plants, role-play . . . etc. all increase the child's scope of understanding and therefore increase the bounds of imagination and creativity.

It is important to reflect on the possibilities in your setting for children to explore and discover for themselves and to consider what you can do to offer an environment where this is possible.

7 Resourcing for creativity

It is not enough to have the perfect space or area for children to create; what is equally as important is what practitioners and leaders choose to fill it with. We know already that children can be creative anywhere, in every area of your play space, indoors and out, and a lot of the time, with minimal resources. However, in this chapter, I will look at some of the key must-have resources for children aged 2 to 5 (and indeed, what we mean when we say this) that will enable and facilitate creative thinking and develop not only their creative tendencies but their sense of autonomy, too. As children get older and toddlers turn into investigative pre-schoolers, their needs, too, inevitably change, and this chapter will look at some of the ways that practitioners can ensure they are giving children a wide range of experiences to cater for their developing skills.

> Aesthetic spaces activate wonder and curiosity, but also remember what is beautiful to you may not be beautiful to the child. With spaces that are aesthetically pleasing, please be aware that it is pointless for a child to have beautiful environment that they cannot explore.
>
> (Carlene Cox-Newton)

This chapter will also explore the theory of loose parts, facilitating creative story-telling as well as, of course, the opportunity for children to experience immersive experiences using paint and other mediums. We will explore some of the techniques that can be used with children who have developed fine and gross motor skills beyond their second year and for those who can retain and recall information, as well as look at the different ways we can offer resources to older children in early years settings and the impact this can have. With the issue of underfunding in the early years

DOI: 10.4324/9781003271710-9

high on the agenda and many settings left struggling to provide high-quality experiences on a budget, it is more important than ever that we focus on the environment that we provide and utilise what funds we do have available investing in good-quality, lasting resources that children will continue to use year after year.

Underpinning knowledge

Before we can begin to think about our environment and the resources that we provide for young children, we must reflect on our values, strengths but also limitations, as these will inevitably have a huge impact on what and how we provide experiences for young children. It is important that leaders have developed a vision with their team that reflects the values they have and the skills and opportunities they want to offer children in their care; only then can they begin to think about what resources they'll need to make these ideas a reality.

With the 2021 early years foundation stage framework revisions making it easier for staff to use their professional judgement for things such as assessment, observation and planning, it is important that staff have sound knowledge and understanding of child development and how children learn in order to form professional judgements and act on them. This means that there is more responsibility on leaders and managers to ensure they keep their staff up-to-date with changing legislation as well as ensure they have ample opportunity for continued professional development. It is important to remember, though, that this responsibility also falls to the practitioners themselves. All too often, we see staff who expect to be told what to do and how to do it with very little initiative. In order to fully develop a team, practitioners have to be given the opportunity to think independently, take a genuine interest in their role and find something that ignites their passion. Often, managers will put staff on courses just to tick a box or to say they have completed their continued professional development quota for the year. This is simply not enough, and our children deserve more. It is not enough to send staff on courses relating to loose parts or storytelling if they don't cascade what they have learnt and embed it within their practice; it will have been a waste of their time and carry no impact for the children they work with. Children deserve passionate, dedicated individuals who want to do their best for the children, and without this, it won't matter about the space or the resources. There is a reason that staff are considered a setting's best asset because without them, there would be very little else. We all have a responsibility to upskill our workforce where we can and ensure that the children, and why we do what we do, remain at the forefront of everything we do.

Accessible resources

When we think about accessible resources, we usually consider where in the environment we put things to ensure children can get them freely and without too much adult intervention. We think critically about any item we do not want children to have free access to and put these out of reach so that in order to have them, children must ask or wait for the adult to set them up. For children to explore their own ideas, they need to have regular and independent access to a variety of different materials, resources, supplies and recyclables, and it is important that practitioners working with young children accept and make this a possibility.

Children from the age of 2 are beginning to understand and, more importantly, accept some boundaries, and supporting children to understand what is expected of them is a vital part of this. When children know what is expected and have consistent boundaries, they are better able to follow instructions and explore resources in a meaningful way. In my first book, *Discover Creativity with Babies*, we explore the idea of accessible resources within the context of baby rooms, allowing children a safe way to select toys and art materials and having a range of objects that are on display, ready to be played with at any time. Although the need for risk assessment doesn't diminish as children get older, the types of resources and materials that we can safely provide for children increases. In many settings, scissors are on display and accessible for children to use freely, woodwork sheds with real tools are used daily and small wooden loose parts are accessible as there is less risk of a child putting it in their mouth. There is no hard and fast rule about what you should and shouldn't have on display, ready to use, or what should be kept out of reach of children in terms of the resources they can use; what is important is that you know your children well and provide them with as much as you can to ensure they have the opportunity to explore their thoughts and make their ideas a reality.

This may look different in each setting, and so it should. No one group of children are the same, and what works for one setting or group of children may not work for another. At our setting, we believe with consistent expectations and boundaries that no resource should be off-limits. Many resources can be safely out for children at all times, without the need for direct supervision; for example, paints, recyclable materials, fabrics and most art resources. Of course, there are some play spaces that must be supervised for the safety of the children; for us, this is our wood-work shed. Children know they must tell an adult if they want to go in and explore, and we ensure that through modelling and meaningful interactions, children know the risks and can manage some of them independently.

For some settings like ours, scissors and glue guns are readily available to our pre-school children should they need them, but I understand this is not the case for everyone. As we have mentioned, it is important not to compare yourself to others but to reflect on what you offer children, their age, level of maturity and understanding, and whether what you do offer is enough to enable them to develop a sense of autonomy and allow them the chance to think creatively.

The theory of loose parts

The theory of loose parts was first coined by Simon Nicholson in the 1970s. It isn't a new concept, and we know that there have always been items and resources that we refer as loose parts; however, many practitioners find it difficult to understand how to use them and what exactly a loose part is. Put simply in terms of Nicholson's theory, a loose part is a variable. Something which has the ability to be many things, much like the way we think about open-ended resources. The two are one in the same, but the way we think about loose parts is often different depending on who you speak to and their knowledge in relation to how loose parts should be offered or used. Many practitioners think that items such as sticks and pebbles are loose parts, and in some cases, they can be; however, what determines this is how a child plays with it. A stick is a stick, it only becomes a loose part when it is turned unintentionally into something else. A pebble is a pebble until the imagination of a child turns it into a turtle or an elephant. This is an important point and is something that some practitioners find difficult. It can be made even more difficult when we set up the environment with a range of natural loose parts and the children appear lost, uninspired and unable to imagine anything other than what it is. Children need to experience different types of resources, too, and often combining them sparks new thinking and a sense of wonder, as seen in this fairy garden invitation to create transient art from Wally's Day Nursery.

It is vital that children have a range of different open-ended resources to interact with in their environment, but just because you have a wicker basket of pinecones or a box of sticks, it doesn't mean you have embedded the theory of loose parts. This can only be done by the children. It isn't enough to provide boxes of natural objects, such as shells or conkers, and say, you 'do loose parts'; staff need to understand and embed a culture of creativity and autonomy in order for the children to use them imaginatively in a variety of ways. For children who are developing their imaginative skills through interaction not only with their peers and adults but with objects, too, it is important that practitioners remain open-minded and allow children to follow their interests, rather than introduce new ones without being invited first.

Little Mini Lighthouse Family Day Care owner Desi reflects on the way she stores resources and has created a loose parts library, where children can go and get resources to enhance their play experiences independently.

Authentic resources

More and more settings are beginning to see the value in authenticity when choosing resources for their play spaces. We have seen that many early years theories involve young children finding out about their world through the use of real items and objects. For most, this means stepping away from the stereotypical brightly coloured plastic usually found in day nurseries and pre-schools and towards a more authentic, real-life experience of day-to-day life. Let's take a minute to reflect on why this is the case, and if it is indeed as beneficial as we believe it to be, why is it that not every setting subscribes to this way of working? In my experience, the main reason more settings haven't adopted authentic resources is lack of confidence and knowledge surrounding why we offer certain opportunities and experiences, and practitioners often feeling lost or overwhelmed in the face of change. For many, the age-old 'why fix something that isn't broken' is a valid justification for why they haven't considered new ways of doing things with young children. If the children like the plastic food, why change it? If they enjoy the car garage, why remove it?

The answers to these questions lie in our own values and what we believe to be the real purpose of our role in early years. If we believe it is our role to extend our children's thinking, develop what they already know into new experiences and provide a rich learning environment for them to discover more about the world they live in, then providing plastic fruit in a brightly coloured plastic kitchen is as far away from a real-life, sensory-rich experience as it can get.

Staff at Pre-School @ St Helens in the Isle of Wight regularly reflect on their environment and how they can incorporate authentic resources whilst exploring real-life experiences the children will be familiar with.

Our role is not to continue to do things just because it's the way it has always been. Practitioners have to reflect and question why they do what they do every day, but the truth of the matter remains that if we want children to experience the world using all their senses, we must give them as many opportunities to do this as possible. This means replacing plastic vegetables with real ones to allow children the chance to feel, smell and perhaps even chop and taste the fruits and vegetables. If offering real foods isn't an option for you, then it's a chance to reflect and come up with creative ways to improve your provision. If budgets are tight, try collecting pebbles or rocks and painting them in the colours of different fruits or using log slices. Why not ask parents to donate something each week in a bid to offset some of the cost of providing real vegetables. At our setting, we use real china and crockery for mealtimes in a bid to resemble a real-life dining experience. Our babies and toddlers, once developmentally able, pour their own drinks from small glass jugs into small mugs rather than brightly coloured plastic cups, and we serve meals and snacks on crockery. Not only does this give children an early sense of responsibility, but it builds the foundation for respect and looking after things. It's also a great way to introduce consequences, something that we talked in detail about in Chapter 3.

Real life and real props have also found their way into home corners and not just through the use of vintage telephones or old cameras. Many settings have begun to appreciate the value in moving away from gendered dressing-up clothes, pink for girls and blue for boys. Traditional princess dresses and superhero costumes have been traded for waistcoats, jackets and long dresses, crowns and swords, whilst some still remain, have been swapped for hats, handbags and costume jewellery, and children are beginning to be shown another way to act out narratives, moving away from a very gendered approach to role play and replacing it with a more natural, autonomous experience. At CheekyRascalz, Amanda Calloway has embedded this ethos within her childminding practice.

Children are able to select a range of items that support the narrative they want recreate, giving them ample opportunity for active learning and high levels of engagement.

Children can choose what to wear and how to wear certain clothing, they can choose a handbag if that's what they want and they are not restricted to certain colours or clothes types. Children need the opportunity to exercise their decision-making skills, and any way that practitioners can do this should be encouraged. In order for children to explore their imaginations, as with loose parts, children need to be given the opportunity to create and recreate roles the way they choose. Whilst there may be value in a princess dress or batman costume for one child, the thinking that is involved when those predesigned dressing-up clothes are no longer available is something of a wonder.

Martine Crowley, a childminder in Wiltshire, also considered how dressing-up clothes can limit children's imagination and now provides fabrics and costume jewellery alongside other common items, such as sunglasses, for the children to investigate and use freely.

Small world and imagination

At a time when sustainability is high on the agenda, I am not suggesting that in order to develop creativity with young children, we have to throw away all plastic toys and resources and replace them with wood resources and found collections; however, it is important to think about the resources we offer and the purpose they serve. The more a toy does, the less there is for a child to do. Many parents now have a plethora of plastic toys adorning living rooms and children's bedrooms, keeping up with the latest trends or trying to support their child's development whilst inadvertently ensuring that any chance of creative thinking and independent thought slowly get taken over by brightly coloured singing and dancing plastic characters. Toys are a children's lived experience, whilst we may subscribe to a different set of values and ethos within our settings, this is something that is difficult to change. We cannot, therefore, decide to remove all the plastic toys and blocks and expect chil-

dren to be happy about it. We can't expect them to play creatively if it isn't something that they have been used to. Practitioners have a vital role here in ensuring that they embed a culture of creative thinking, striking a balance of familiar and natural resources. If we want children to think creatively, we must give them the skills, engagement and opportunities to do so. A simple way to do this is to combine several elements in creating small worlds, keeping some of our much-loved open-ended plastic resources but combining them with other, more natural elements.

Abbie-May Moore from Scallywags Nursery in Chelmsford used her trip to Iceland to engage and further the children's knowledge. By using small figures, glacier bricks and books to complement the photographs from her trip, children were able to play creatively, introduce their own narratives and share in the awe and wonder of her trip.

I think it is SO important to share your own experiences with your children, so they can understand and trust you as a key person, and for you to learn alongside them too.

Within the environment at Scallywags, practitioners set up small-world invitations for the children based on their interests. Arranged on open, low shelves, children can access them independently and are encouraged to reset the spaces when their play has finished.

A plastic, predesigned car garage can be only one thing. It will never be a mountain for dinosaurs or a café for the dollies to visit; it is, by design, a garage for cars. The role of the practitioner here is to think about ways we can engage children in expressing their own ideas about how a garage could be built, perhaps using toilet rolls stacked on top of each other or using the blocks to create parking spaces. When we think about imaginative play, it is easy to see how we can incorporate more natural, environmentally friendly items, such as bark or logs for a pond and wooden blocks to create bridges and castles. Good-quality small wooden people are fantastic additions to invitations to think creatively and imagine different worlds, but again, you can utilise some of what you have without throwing away everything and having to buy new. For example, plastic dinosaurs provide the perfect finishing touch to a Jurassic land, fairy figurines or china animals picked up from boot sales can be used in woodland or fairy gardens, and children can create their own using photographs of themselves and their friends on DUPLO blocks.

Hayley Dyke, owner of Little Wise Owls Childminding, thinks creatively when offering small-world opportunities, ensuring that children have the freedom to choose how and what to play with alongside well-thought-out resources.

I try to have a few different learning opportunities to meet the different ages/stages of the children in my setting, that's why they always look quite busy.

Dolls have been a staple of the early years role play environment for as long as any of us can remember, and long may they continue to be. As with any resource, it is how they are placed within the environment to encourage children to use them imaginatively and give children the opportunity to recreate and imitate roles from home. They are also great for introducing and exploring emotions and empathy as practitioners talk to children about how to hold them and care for them.

Block play and construction

Building blocks, wooden and foam bricks, builder's bricks, and wood offcuts can be used to create some of the best learning opportunities for toddlers and pre-school children and is a resource that no early years setting should be without. They provide for children the opportunity to explore concepts such as height, length and weight as well as mathematical concepts of shape and size. Toddlers should already know about a range of objects and their properties, and as their brains expand and their experience of the world grows, they will encounter their first blocks. These introductory experiences include vital learning, such as how heavy a particular block is and what it feels like depending on what it's made of, and they may begin to carry them around with them (further exploring their need to transport objects). We can also see cause and effect and schematic play as it develops, so making sure children have buckets, wheelbarrows, large pans or even bowls to fill and then empty will allow them to explore their thinking. Children are fantastic at using blocks and loose parts together to create their own structures, something that Zoe Clark has observed with the children at Aylesbury Vale Academy Pre-School.

This is a loose parts creation from a three year old, who has a real 'eye' for making various sized models. He is passionate about vehicles and in this photograph, he has made a car to demonstrate how it moves, he added a lever 'It's like this see, up and down'. He spent 45 minutes carefully arranging the loose parts, collecting parts from all over the pre-school. He knew exactly how it should look and proudly demonstrated his understanding by explaining it to everyone who walked in.

In this example, we can see how loose parts, block play and children's early literacy skills can be combined when children have the freedom to choose and reflective practitioners value schematic and interest-led play.

Socially, block play contributes to the development of self-confidence and esteem, as they learn how to stack blocks and build towers, they feel a sense of accomplishment, often wanting to show those around them. Practitioners can support children by commenting on their ideas, not interfering but offering suggestions and comments to extend their play and their early language and communication skills. As children grow

and develop the ability to communicate effectively and extend their ideas themselves, practitioners can ask meaningful open-ended questions to encourage children's creative thinking.

Practitioners at Little Learners in Corby know how important the resources they choose are in promoting the notion of the environment as the third teacher. They create spaces of awe and wonder whilst offering a range of purposeful opportunities.

This will also give the children opportunity to use and explore narratives alongside others. Four-year-olds have the added communicative ability that younger children may not possess yet, meaning their play is often more developed and somewhat organised. This is where block play and added accessories can extend their ideas as they share them with friends and build on those early relationships with others as well as develop their understanding of more complex concepts such as classifying, sequencing and making patterns.

Malleable materials

Using malleable materials with young children helps to develop fundamental skills relating to materials and their properties. Many early years practitioners can make salt dough, play dough and other forms of dough without having to look for a recipe, and this is a testament to the importance of dough when working with children. Toddlers should have daily access to media that they can investigate and explore freely, and ensuring that malleable play is a part of this is vital.

Neston Farm Nursery provide malleable materials in their outdoor environment for children not only to explore their tactile sense but to develop and use their environment to extend their creative thinking.

For those who may have purchased this book as an introduction to creative play with young children and have perhaps never come across the word, *malleable* refers to any material that children can easily manipulate. Something that develops their fine motor skills and that can be transformed if the children choose, through the use of tools or combining different elements. Some of the most common and readily available malleable materials include the following:

■ Play dough

■ Clay

■ Sand

■ Water

■ Mud

You'll notice that these materials are available within the environment already, perhaps outdoors, as is the case for mud and water, or are extremely cheap to make using only a few ingredients.

Many settings have areas where malleable play is encouraged, often ensuring that a variety of tools are accessible, and some even have provision for children to make their own dough using flour, water and other important additions, such as herbs and spices. This is great if you have the space and budget to ensure these ingredients are always available, but if not, there is still opportunity to offer this play and keep costs down. Many settings have taken advantage of the guidance that states a consumable charge can be passed on to parents of funded 3- and 4-year-olds. This means that there is some scope to continue to provide resources that often need replenishing. If this isn't something that you feel able to do at your setting, parents are usually more than happy to donate; you could send out a list of wanted items to parents as part of a newsletter, making sure you explain the benefits of offering such resources daily.

Another fantastic malleable resource for young children is clay. Although it can't be made or found, like some of the others, it offers many benefits so should be offered where possible and is safe under supervision from 18 months. It is important to remember that the crucial factor when offering any type of resource is the child. In the case of dough, clay or mud, the child's interests and fascinations must be listened to and their stage of development kept at the forefront.

This is something that Little Learners in Corby do particularly well. Drawing on their children's current interests, they present photographs and wooden blocks alongside clay and various other resources as they invite the children to create their own masterpieces.

It is not enough to offer these materials and expect the children to know what to do with them; this is particularly important at the time of writing in the context of the coronavirus pandemic where children have been away from early years settings and spent prolonged periods of time at home. The experiences children have had will differ greatly between families, and this needs to be taken into account when considering our environment and what we provide within it. Children cannot be expected to create clay sculptures at age 3 without

having had the repeated opportunity to explore and experience the material and its properties first. Children who are hesitant and perhaps unfamiliar with sensory invitations can be offered tools to encourage their exploration indirectly, and offering water alongside clay or dough can change its look and texture, further adding to the sensory experience.

Art-based materials

When we think about creativity, many practitioners automatically think about the paints and collage materials they provide for young children on a regular basis, but as we have seen, being creative is about so much more than marks on paper. This is perhaps why I have chosen to leave these types of resources until the end of the chapter. Creativity, as we have seen, is about having the freedom of thought, imagination and perception; developing a variety of skills; having time to formulate plans and ideas; and having the right resources in order to make something of value to the child. In order to express their ideas, children benefit from a wide range of art materials that are age-appropriate and accessible, and it is the role of the practitioner to offer as many varieties as they can to ensure this is possible. Implements for mark-making, such as pencils, pens and chalks, should be available throughout the environment, alongside clipboards, giving the children the opportunity to move with their drawings or creations. If they write a shopping list, they may like to take it when they go to the shops; having fixed areas of provision limits this opportunity of movement for young children and may stifle their creative thinking.

The way in which we provide art resources for children from the age of 2 is different in some respects to what we offer babies and younger children. Whilst there are still safety considerations and risk assessments for some products, with their growing independence and skill alongside their increased communicative abilities, it is often easier to allow certain resources to be accessible to children all the time. From the age of around 20 months, children at Wally's Day Nursery have access to a wide range of resources that they have the freedom to use as and when they choose. Staff set up invitations to play and explore based on the children's current interests, and these are always optional for the children to engage with or not. Paint is stored where children can access it independently alongside paintbrushes and other mark-making tools. Our toddlers have shelves at their height to store other materials, such as coloured rice and pasta, alongside PVA glue, sprinkles, feathers and an array of other collage bits and bobs.

As children get older and move through our rooms, the resources available to them increase, too, and invitations to create often use real life as a source of inspiration, whether that is objects, photographs or things based on experiences the children have had, such as a visit to the pumpkin patch.

As I have already pointed out, our pre-school children have access to glue guns and scissors as well as a range of other art materials, stored by colour for the children to see what is available to them but also to aid them in putting their resources back on the shelves.

Higher-risk resources or those that require closer supervision, such as inks and fabric paints, are great for older pre-school children as they develop the ability to listen further and challenge their thinking. By providing resources like inks, Modroc, plaster and different types of paint, children really can create something magical. Practitioners may prefer to stay within the realms of what they know, through their lack of confidence with new skills or because of management limitations or budgets. Providing poster or powder paints, glue, Pritt sticks and other common materials in many cases still allows the child to be creative, but the ability to explore can be limited. There are infinite possibilities in these resources, but by respecting children's abilities and giving them the opportunity to investigate watercolours, acrylics, inks and materials for sculpture and other forms of art, children learn new ways of art making and develop skills beyond simply painting a picture. If this seems like a new concept, allowing children as young as 3 to explore and create using adult mediums, such as acrylics and clay, I implore you to reflect on why you think this way and ask yourself why not.

Recyclables

The idea of sustainability and doing what we can to protect the planet is becoming more of a priority for early years settings across the UK and elsewhere. Reducing waste and thinking about the types of resources that we offer to young children takes a lot of consideration, and if you are not part of the eco community, it might seem like a difficult task. It is easy to get started by recycling some of your unwanted cardboard and fabrics, and without much thinking, you'll soon get into the habit of collecting interesting items that can be repurposed. For those with a large garden, composting food waste is a great way to teach children about their world and how we can reduce the amount we throw away. In the context of creativity, though, there are some much simpler ways that we can use what we no longer need to encourage looking after the planet and making something new and original with what we have. Asking parents for recycling ensures that there is usually always a steady stream of new resources coming into the setting, from cardboard boxes to play with to cereal boxes for junk modelling.

Andrea Booth, owner of Andrea's Childcare in Rushden, knows all too well the importance and benefits of using recyclable materials with young children to develop their creativity and imaginative thinking. She provides a range of resources collected, saved and donated for the children to use on a daily basis. Boxes, different tube sizes, packing material (please always supervise young children and discard anything not suitable) and even the cupholders from coffee shops make a great free resource that young children can use in creative ways depending on their current level of development or interests.

The easiest way to store recyclable material is in large buckets or bins; this gives the children a sense of responsibility as they can bring items from home and can put them where they go independently. At Wally's, we have three large bins for fabrics, cardboard and plastic.

The children have learnt the difference and can sort the recycling into the bins ready for them to use as and when they need it. By having them accessible, children can use them for projects, such as sculpture and modelling, or to support them in their role play as they make new clothes from the fabrics they like. It also means parents are supporting their children indirectly by ensuring they always have well-stocked recycling.

It doesn't always have to be large items either; when we consider recycling many simply think about the boxes they can reuse. Other resources that can be reused include mediums such as charcoal or flowers; they are fantastic for children to investigate. The marks children can make with charcoal and the observation of what happens when it is wet or gets smudged, and the colours children can explore, making paint or using fabric for printing, gives a whole new life to unwanted or past-their-best flowers. Rubber bands are also a worthwhile addition to any provision for the development of fine motor skills, and staff can ask for donations when they are running low on specific items.

Immersive experiences

One last point that I feel deserves its place here is the concept of immersive experiences for young children. We have already explored why this is the case in Chapter 6 and the importance of providing opportunities that allow children to be truly immersed in an experience. As practitioners, it is important that we acknowledge the benefit of being in the moment at a particular activity. Immersive experiences can be anything from sand, water, paint and mud to less-obvious prolonged periods of time at an activity of the child's choosing.

Children at Wallys Pre-School have a large immersive sandpit alongside the sand shack to fully experience the joy of sand between their toes.

Young children are also given the freedom to engage with media in a way that suits them, offering whole body experiences if appropriate, alongside meaningful interactions.

In this chapter, we have discussed the resources that children need in order to develop their creative thinking, and with that in mind, when we think about immersive experiences for young children, we are specifically thinking about those times when children have the opportunity to get in and really engage with the idea of a lot and more. Children need the freedom to use to excess, and as practitioners, it is important that we understand the value of this. I understand that for some, the need to keep replacing resources such as paint can be difficult, especially when budgets are already stretched, but there are ways that children can still benefit from this type of play without breaking the bank. Mud from the outdoors is readily available and can be offered in abundance alongside water. Sand is also relatively cheap and, if contained in large immersive pits, will last long enough to allow children the chance to really explore it.

Top ten must-have resources for 2–5s

1   Natural collected treasures

■ Why? Because if children have collected them, they will be more likely to engage with them for prolonged periods.

2   Dolls

■ Why? Because young children need the opportunity to role play and recreate, and those with younger siblings can imitate actions from home. They are also great for embedding emotion play and empathy.

3   Art materials

■ Why? Because children should have a range of materials to create and explore their ideas by creating representations of things that are important to them.

4   Recycled fabrics/cardboard/plastics

■ Why? Recycled boxes give children ample opportunities to explore schemas, and other recycled items can be used in junk modelling at an age-appropriate level.

5   Containers/buckets

■ Why? Thinking back to schematic play, children love to empty and fill containers and transport objects. They should have plenty of buckets or containers to ensure this is possible.

6   Selection of good-quality small-world animals and people

■ Why? Young children cannot imagine animals or people if they don't have objects of reference or knowledge to draw from. Giving children farm animals, dinosaurs and sea creatures as part of meaningful invitations to play will develop their understanding of the world they live in.

7   Deconstructed authentic role play objects

■ Why? Children should be given the opportunity to imagine and imitate others with authentic real-life items to develop their understanding of themselves and their autonomy as well as those around them.

8   Immersive opportunities

■ Why? Children love to immerse themselves in experiences. Providing enough sand to get in and dig deep provides opportunities not possible in a sand tray. The same can be said for water and other immersive play, such as painting. Think creatively about how you can offer children the experience of lots.

9   Blocks/construction opportunities

■ Why? Block play is vital for children's development. It provides so many opportunities for children to experiment with their ideas, build at height where possible (using step ladders) and create their own original structures.

10   Malleables

■ Why? Providing a range of malleable materials ensures that children not only have the opportunity to develop their fine and gross motor skills and express their ideas in a tangible way but that they have the chance to strengthen vital muscles in their hands that they will eventually need for writing.

This is by no means an exhaustive list of resources for toddlers and older children up to the age of 5. It would be impossible to list them all and their respective benefits. The key in resourcing for toddlers and pre-school children is diversity of opportunities and giving children the time they need to think about their ideas and how to represent them, alongside meaningful interactions and purposefully designed play spaces and invitations to explore.

8 **Exploring outdoors**

> When you make it possible for children to discover their own inner radiance, you provide them with a key to illuminate the world.
>
> (Laura Brothwell)

It is often the case that being outdoors evokes a range of emotions in all of us. The freedom that being outdoors, surrounded by nature brings is second to none, which is why it is so important in the lives of our little ones. At an age when they are exploring and learning about the world in a very physical way, it is vital that we give children the opportunity to spend free time outdoors, doing what they choose alongside adults who they can trust and who trust them. Being outdoors is important for children of any age, but in an increasingly technological world with more and more children living sedentary lifestyles, it is more important than ever to ensure that our children are taking the time to slow down and get outside and spending as much time as possible in nature. This chapter will look at how we can ensure those from the age of 2 in early years settings, home-based childcare and pre-schools are getting the most from the outdoors and exploring the range of opportunities that can be facilitated outside. This includes woodland learning and the ethos of forest schools, as well as the rise of nature-deficit disorder and children with additional needs being identified which in turn affects the way young children can express themselves and develop the confidence to think for themselves, take risks and manage challenge independently.

In this chapter, we will explore some of the ways practitioners can make the most of their time with young children outside, regardless of the space they have available. It will also look at the lasting impact of not experiencing the outdoors freely in the years following infancy and what practitioners can do to ensure that they give children the best experience of the outdoors.

DOI: 10.4324/9781003271710-10

Why is the outdoors so important?

We know that the outdoors can illicit learning above and beyond what can be replicated in an indoor environment. There are several reasons for this, but perhaps the most important is that outdoors, children can experience the world using all their senses with very little interference from adults. Often free of the same restrictions that are imposed on children indoors, they have the freedom and autonomy to engage with a range of natural experiences on their terms at their pace. Children need to experience the world they live in, and the only way to do this is to go outside. With an increase in the number of young children who have access to technological devices and spend more and more of their time indoors, it is more important than ever that children are encouraged to go outside. Parents often don't see the harm in allowing children screen time; however, as the amount of time spent watching television or demanding the iPad increases, the time remaining for play outdoors decreases. Sadly, even when time isn't the issue, children prefer their sedentary lifestyles. As practitioners and advocates for what is best for young children in their earliest years, it is vital that we spend as much time outside with children, allowing them the freedom to explore at their own pace their interests and fascinations.

Children have an innate curi-osity, a need to find out about things and challenge themselves, their bodies and their thinking. 'Over time, research has found that the more variety of outdoor learning approaches children experience, the greater the diversity and learning potential there is for the child' (Johnson & Watts, 2019:47).

Outdoor learning or forest school?

Outdoor learning within the UK is fundamentally different to that in countries such as those in the Scandinavian region, Denmark and Finland. The reason for this is that our culture and society are also fundamentally different; however, as Slade et al. (2013:66) argue, even with 'declining access to and engagement with the natural environment', the movement has 'gained momentum in the UK in recent years'. More and more settings are finding the benefits of being outdoors with children far outweigh what they can achieve indoors, and so many have taken their children outdoors full time, rebranding as outdoor nurseries where children spend most of their day enjoying the elements, connecting with nature. This is particularly true in the context of the coronavirus pandemic. At a time when being outdoors was deemed safer, lowering the transmission rate of the virus was a priority for many settings, and they spent time reflecting and altering their environments, not only to cater for the needs of the children but to ensure that at the time, they were doing what they could to keep the children safe. In doing so, many rediscovered the beauty of the outdoors and the rich learning that takes place there, making their changes permanent.

Some settings get caught up in the type of provision they have or don't have and the purpose it serves. Settings don't have to have a qualified forest school leader to enjoy being outdoors with young children, exploring with them and developing their skills in the outdoors. Forest school provision is different to outdoor learning in that settings using the forest school title, must have a qualified forest school practitioner and follow a set of guiding principles. A forest school has the ability to encompass all the elements needed to develop early creativity and critical thinking by emphasizing 'the "rich possibilities" that arise when children can initiate their own activities and follow them through without interference or direction from an adult.'

Neston Farm Nursery in Wiltshire, UK, spend their days outside in nature. Children have long uninterrupted periods of play and benefit from playing and learning alongside the animals that they help to care for.

It is important to recognise, though, that it is not just forest schools that can provide this for children. When we go outside with young children, some practitioners feel that they have to have several objectives and plans in place in order to feel they have achieved something with the children they work with, but often, this is far from the case and goes against what we know about learning outdoors. Countless health and safety concerns, risk assessments and red tape culture has meant that settings are staying within the boundaries of their provision gardens, missing the opportunity to get out into nature within the community and show children their wider world. Being outdoors is much more than paperwork, and often, the best outcomes are those that occur naturally. The experience of the outdoors can be somewhat clouded by leaders in early years who misjudge the importance of nature in children's development, but it is our role to advocate for children and give them the opportunities they deserve. Whether that is during prolonged periods of outdoor play within the setting, in our gardens and outside spaces, in the community or within the realm of true forest school. What is important is not what we call it but that we continue to do it every day to ensure children can experience the joys of nature and freedom to explore the vastness of space, activating all their senses.

Parental engagement

One of the biggest hurdles to outdoor play in early years is the attitudes of parents and their engagement with the importance of outdoor play at the setting. Parents are their child's first educators; it stands to reason that some of their beliefs and values will be passed on to their children. Whilst for the most part this is a good thing, parents have a key role in setting expectations, teaching empathy and supporting their children in language development; we have seen that parents can also pass on their attitudes towards outdoors and getting messy.

We have all faced parents who believe going outside causes colds, who believe that children should be kept inside if they are unwell and who refuse to bring appropriate clothing for their child so that they cannot go out to play, get muddy or get wet, and have generally what all children need, a great day. This not only is detrimental to children's experience in early years but sends messages about the outdoors to children that are not grounded in truth and serve to disrupt their natural curiosity about the world around them.

One way to engage parents and get them excited about the opportunities that exist outdoors is to invite them along to accompany trips. This is something that staff at Scallywags Nursery Chelmsford did with great success.

It was a perfect chance for our practitioners to build relationships with our families and share our vision of promoting outdoor learning and play.

By sharing outdoor experiences with parents in a hands-on approach, they will begin to see the benefits that, as early years practitioners, we know and appreciate. They will be able to spend time with their child outdoors with their peers and observe them and the fun they have. Practitioners can then challenge their thinking and encourage them to reflect on the impact their actions have on their children. If a parent avoids messy activities and keeps a clean house where children are not allowed to touch or make mess, children will naturally be less likely to engage in this type of play in settings.

REFLECTION

As a team, think about some of the ways you encourage parents to engage with outdoor play.

Is there anything that you could do to improve this?

Consider the following:

- Sending home activities for parents to complete with their child; this could be doing a nature walk, collecting interesting treasures or going on a listening walk.

- Finding information and distributing it to parents on the benefits of the outdoors.

- Inviting parents along to stay and play sessions where they can see for themselves the children playing and exploring freely in the outdoors.

- Running some parent's workshops where they have the opportunity to play uninterrupted in nature if it is feasible. Often, individuals just need to reconnect with the earth to see the benefits it offers.

Be mindful of parents who may not have the means to provide warm clothing for their child and offer support. Often, parents donate waterproof suits or wellies that their child has outgrown that can be offered to families to ensure no child misses out.

Practitioners outdoors

As Rogoff points out, 'children in all communities are cultural participants' (Rogoff, 2003:10); this suggests a reciprocal relationship between the child and the individuals that they come into contact with on a regular basis. It does, however, depend on whether or not those individuals view the child as a participant, as failure to recognize this would lead to a lack of communication and understanding. This is demonstrated more clearly by Hedegaard and Fleer (2013:7) when they talk of how 'a caregiver will approve and help a child reach for an object the child desires, or the caregiver will do the opposite, depending on both the traditions and values of a particular society' (Hedegaard & Fleer, 2013:7); this is something which is evidenced in many forest school contexts, where children from different cultures and societies will react in different ways depending on the way they have been brought up.

Practitioners have a responsibility to reflect on their own ideas about outdoor play and how it supports the holistic development of the child, and they must think critically about how they perceive the outdoors and the opportunities that are made possible. Similar concerns can arise around adult attitudes and the effect they have on children when staff refuse to go out to play when it's cold or raining. Perhaps they don't have a coat that day, didn't bring their wellies or would prefer to stay inside. This is not helpful for several reasons. Children need staff who are curious, are good role models and can be active play partners. One thing leaders can do is to ensure that their staff are well prepared with the correct clothing for outdoor learning. Another, and perhaps very key point, is to recruit staff who share the same ethos and values as the setting. Practitioners who are passionate about the benefits of outdoors will remember their coat and wellies and be willing to go outdoors in all weathers. Seeing this enthusiasm for outdoor play will encourage the children to want to go outside and explore no matter what the weather is doing.

Here, Wendy Hamley from The Forest Approach discusses how she supports others and promotes creativity in the outdoors.

A forest/outdoor environment can promote development of self-awareness by peers providing opportunities for children to build wonderful, shared experiences to challenge themselves and build curiosity, discovery, and a way to bring nature into our creative minds.

Physical activities such as tree climbing that support awareness of physical self or reflective activities that encourage children to analyse their successes and failures. It is not bad to fail; it is a learning curve to achieve and one we definitely need to progress and overcome failure. This also strengthens the children's muscles to build their creative skills. Self-awareness is the ability to know one's emotions, strengths, weaknesses, values, beliefs, and goals and recognise their impact on others while using own feelings to make decisions and make ideas. Nature has the ability to evoke creative ways of thinking with natural sources, using sticks, stones, leaves, mud and so much more.

Children will be given plenty of opportunities to promote creative skills within a forest environment, gaining knowledge in working in different aged and sized groups. Play will develop verbal and non-verbal communication which will support the development of social skills. Motivated child led environments and involving children in the process promotes motivation as they allow children to explore their own interests and learn in a way that suits their learning style all the time ensuring that sessions are kept as flexible as possible and encouraging children to take ownership of and lead activities. This will support development of motivation as it will give a sense of achievement. Children can successfully motivate themselves to achieve their goals and it is important to have good role models to enhance this.

It is clear from The Forest Approach that the role of the adults involved with young children when outdoors is a hands-on partnership. Working alongside the children to support them when they need it and to encourage them to challenge themselves even when they lack the self-confidence to do something independently.

There is also an element of guiding children in their exploits. Whilst most of their play outdoors is free and children should be allowed to choose how to spend their time, sometimes children benefit from strong role models to extend their learning and ideas. This is something Martine Crowley is mindful of in her practice with children outdoors, sharing their experiences with them.

Leading by example whether it's me or older children in the setting helps children to think creatively and from this base they begin to build their own picture of the world.

The outdoors spark ideas, and these ideas are sometimes reflected in activities back at the setting. For one little boy, having found a frog during a trip to the woodland pond, it sparked an invitation to represent frogs with watercolours once back inside.

Exploring the benefits of being outdoors

We know that the benefits of children spending prolonged time outdoors are endless. From the sensory experience of nature to the calming effect of being outside, being in nature is vital for all aspects of development, and we have seen through research that this is the case for children as well as adults.

Many settings are lucky enough to have a large open space for the children onsite or even separate play spaces for each age group, and what a fantastic opportunity this provides. Staff can create different areas, features and play invitations for the children on a daily basis or as and when reflection dictates, which means that children are kept interested and always have something that stimulates and challenges them. However, even those settings who have large gardens and spaces for the children to explore outside have to be mindful about the opportunities they provide. It isn't enough just to have the space available. As I have mentioned, it is what staff do with it that keeps the children interested, and the ability to reflect on what is being provided each day or week as well as having resources available to extend children's ideas ensures that a variety of opportunities are being offered. Having space for children that is freely accessible at all times is great, but there can be one downside that many practitioners and sometimes leaders, too, don't appreciate, and that is the missed opportunities for play and exploration outside of the setting. This is something that in her childminding practice, Martine Crowley ensures is not the case, taking the children out regularly to local areas of interest.

For settings who don't have access to a large area or those with certain types of outdoor provision, such as artificial grass, concrete patios or other terrain that can offer challenges, it becomes even more important not only that children explore the space they have but that practitioners and leaders see the benefits of going out into the community and experiencing different outdoor environments and places of interest.

One of the unique selling points of the day nursery I manage is the opportunities we provide for the children outside the setting. We consider ourselves very lucky to have a central location within our community. Close to the town centre and local transport links, we have families who come from within the town and those who travel to us from further afield. We cater for children from 3 months to 5 years which means we offer not only fee-paying places but also places for children who are entitled to two-year funding and those on the universal and extended 3- and 4-year-old funding. Families can walk, use public transport or drive to our setting, and because of where we are situated, we can be accessed by everyone. In the following case study, I have outlined what we provide on a regular basis to ensure that we continue to build on the children's experiences and give them a variety of opportunities in their early years with us.

Case study: Wally's Day Nursery

Our setting is not purpose-built and has a small outdoor area across two levels. The top level (directly accessed by our babies and pre-school children) is laid with artificial grass and features a small pond, planters and climbing equipment whilst the lower level is made up of a largely concrete area and an alleyway connecting the three buildings we have. We have utilised the space to incorporate a sensory path (built by one of our parents) and have recently transformed what was our mud kitchen into a water garden, again, using donated items, bricks and pebbles. Of course, I would love nothing more than a beautiful, detached setting with acres of land for the children to explore and spend their days in nature; however, this is just not possible for us, as we are on an industrial estate in a busy town. We are aware, however, of the vital role nature plays in young children's development, and therefore, we go above and beyond many settings in our local area to ensure our children have fantastic opportunities both at nursery and in the community.

We have two successful outdoor programmes, our nature babies for under 3s and our woodland learning sessions for our over 3s. We know that children need to play and have uninterrupted time to experience their world, developing their spatial awareness, skills in movement and sensory stimulation. Our nature babies and woodland learning sessions provide all our children with just that; uninterrupted time to explore outdoors. Our toddler unit, which caters for children from 18 months, have weekly opportunities to spend a prolonged amount of uninterrupted time outdoors, whether using our outdoor learning environment for the morning/afternoon or visiting local places of interest in the community, such as a local park, open space or our private woodland. Whilst there, we use a hands-free philosophy, whereby children are free to explore on their own terms, free from handholding, prams or reigns. In order to develop critical thinking and problem-solving skills, children need to be able to experience the world for themselves without the restrictions often placed on them by adults.

Our pre-school children benefit from our woodland learning sessions, weekly sessions for groups of up to twenty-six children where we visit our private woodland to explore, experience and simply be in nature. The sessions are based around the emerging interests and skills of the children and include nature-based creative activities, physical challenges, pond dipping and cooking on the campfire after foraging for ingredients. These sessions are rarely pre-planned, unless we have to take equipment for cooking, and we take our cues from the children. Occasionally, we will use what the children have been interested in at the setting and extend it out in the woods or fields with invitations to explore further, but if the children find their own fascinations, we will always follow their lead. By allowing children unstructured time outdoors, they have the opportunity to experience at their own pace the rich sensory input that nature provides. It not only encourages curiosity, exploration, understanding and self-regulation but provides the ideal learning environment for all children, regardless of their age or abilities as all their senses can be engaged.

As well as regular access to the woods, we appreciate and value the experiences that can be provided through educational trips. Like most settings in the UK, at Wally's, we have the concept of cultural capital at the forefront of our practice. Ensuring that children get the best possible start, regardless of their background or previous experiences. This means getting to know the children and their lived experiences and working alongside them to show them the awe and wonder in the world. Often in line with the children's interests to further their understanding and extend vocabulary around the subject, in the autumn, we visit the pumpkin patch for the children to choose their own pumpkins, and we often take them to seasonal events, too. Getting out into the community is important for the children to support their understanding of the wider world and their place within it. If we feel a particular outing or experience will benefit the children, we will do what we can to ensure it happens. We have recently started taking a small group of children with additional needs to the local donkey sanctuary once a week as part of our animal therapy programme. The children benefit from time with the animals, grooming them and finding out what they like to eat. Each week, the children choose what to bring as a treat for the animals, and we use our time with them to learn new vocabulary. For children with poor physical skills and muscle tone, riding the donkeys also gives them an opportunity to build core strength and work at holding on independently.

It is important to us that children have the opportunity to experience the world they live in wholeheartedly, alongside practitioners who know how important it is for children's holistic development. We take pride in the staff team we have and their dedication to the children they work with, often using their own lived experiences as a way to connect with them and share their knowledge of the world alongside them.

In the earlier case study, I hope you can begin to understand that often, it is not the size of the space you have but what you do with it, and when you face limitations, perhaps in terms of size or material, that you reflect on ways you can use the local community and offer children valuable experiences and opportunities.

Restricted access to outdoors

If children live sheltered from their environment and are raised without interaction or, indeed, exploration of the outdoors, they will inevitably be unable to connect with nature, as it has no meaning to them. At a time when many don't have access to gardens or parents are juggling several jobs with the rising cost of living, children are suffering, and their opportunities for play outdoors is limited. We know the effects of spending a prolonged amount of time in front of screens, and we are seeing the impact on children in our settings. Tell-tale signs that children are left largely to their own devices at home include those with limited physical skills, those who prefer to stay away from physical challenges and children who don't possess age-appropriate abilities such as jumping or balancing.

Often, settings in highly sought-after areas with large grounds charge a premium to cover running and staff costs of such large nurseries, and this would price out many parents, resulting in them having to choose second- or third-option settings closer to home or the one with the lowest hourly rate in the area to manage the costs of providing childcare and maintaining a home. This doesn't have to mean that children miss out, but it can be the case that if the setting chosen doesn't place high value on outdoor experiences, children can experience reduced time outdoors than if they were at alternative settings. As we have seen, it is the role of practitioners working in early years settings and the managers and leaders of those settings to look at ways they can embrace the outdoors and provide ways for children to reap the benefits.

Bright Stars Nursery love to enhance their outdoor area regularly to ensure that all children have access to a high-quality environment with opportunities to develop their creativity.

In the following case study, Laura Brothwell from Stone Hen Childcare acknowledges the importance of keeping children connected to nature and ensuring that in doing so, we can keep their childhood intact in an increasingly disconnected, technological world.

Case study: Stone Hen Childcare

Our core focus has always been connecting children to nature, supporting a collective vision of sustainable education – not just ecological sustainability but the sustainability of childhood. A lifelong love for learning will be instilled in children who are free to express themselves, communicating and exploring their own ideas and learning within a self-driven process.

We believe creative critical thinking is a core skill; liberating children to unconditionally love their own unique strengths and weaknesses, builds the confidence to think out of the box, applying resilience and innovation when working towards accomplishing new skills and intentions. To provide children with the best foundations for creativity to flourish, we feel that acknowledging all eight senses within the early years, will support children's holistic development; thus providing them with their own unique ability to familiarise and express their creative self through a beautiful array of avenues on their journey throughout childhood.

Nature offers a sensory rich learning environment, accommodating all eight senses. Bursting with open space, fresh air, natural light and an ever-changing canvas, artistic expression is entwined and inspired within all aspects and avenues of nature. Creativity is a frequency at which children resonate much better than the majority of adults. Play in any capacity is a form of creative expression, the ability to be inspired comes from the sub/consciousness of connecting to oneself and one's environment. We see a heightened burst of creativity in children when immersed in nature compared to that when exploring within the classroom.

We believe immersed in nature, whether it be a garden or a large natural space children are granted a sense of freedom to discover themselves and unlock their inner creative flow, demonstrating the magic of childhood, bursting with opportunity, ideas, wonder and beauty.

One way we support this is by utilising the seasons which provide cyclic change amongst the landscapes with new bursts of inspiration, a common familiarisation, storytelling, culture and diverse opportunity.

We integrate connection to nature within daily practice by inviting the children to develop their own relationships with the nature and the provision garden, cultivating new growth and magic, therefore children build their own creative story of action through a sense of place that is developed by their community and peers. We maintain the land, grow and harvest produce, build and implement interventions to support wildlife, practice mindfulness and meditation, construct and design dens, dreaming nooks and soundscapes . . . alongside adventuring to the local landscapes beyond the setting boundaries. We utilise our landscapes to harvest media and resources for our creative play and discovery. Herbs, flowers, water collection, soil, twigs, sticks, fruits, vegetables, berries, branches, – in order to make paints, loose parts, construction tools, seasonal crafts, structures, mark making tools, cooking dishes, sensory enhancements to playdough and malleable experiences, mud kitchen and role play, sound scapes, we're constantly experimenting and exploring. In doing so children develop a reciprocal relationship with the land, understanding the benefits of nature, the opportunity of the beauty, valuing their ongoing hard work, finding joy within the magic of a garden – tuning into all eight senses and liberating their creative impulse. At Stone Hen we not only value the creative expression of children, but equally value our own fluid pedagogy as a form of creative expression to enlighten and inspire holistic learning and development.

It is abundantly clear from this case study that Laura places extremely high importance on the outdoors, and ensuring all children connect with nature in a way that is sustainable and supports their holistic development and quality of experience. We should all, as early years practitioners, seek to share this passion for outdoor learning so that all children can experience the richness of nature alongside staff they trust.

Sensory input

We have already seen the vast array of benefits for young children from being outside, and research shows that children of all ages need a sensory-rich environment that features a variety of textures, temperatures, colours, smells and sounds. Something that is always on offer at Nina's Nursery High Lane.

This can be somewhat replicated indoors through providing opportunities for children that will excite and keep them interested, but almost all will be artificial. Artificial lights, plants in pots, plastic texture mats and a well-placed essential oils diffuser cannot replace what the outdoors has in abundance.

Being outdoors with young children can be a fascinating experience. This is especially the case if it is not something that they are used to; for example, if they live in a flat or area that is largely urban, children can become quickly overwhelmed with the availability of space and freedom. Toddlers and pre-school children, who may have had some experience of the outdoors, begin to explore their senses and, because of their increased communication skills, can begin to describe what they feel. There is more opportunity for listening outdoors, too, as practitioners are unlikely to be bound by routines and timings, not to mention the lack of irrelevant background noise outdoors. Birds, trees, the sound of water trickling into a pond, these sounds within nature have a calming effect on young children and produce higher levels of engagement with adults and peers.

A great invitation to explore terrain is to encourage the children to practise earthing; the act of making direct contact with the earth. This is a particularly powerful way of connecting children to the sensory input of grass (maybe it is wet from the rain), puddles, cold mud and other textures of nature. Some children will need to support to engage with this if it is not something they are used to. This will take time, and as we know children learn from repetition, repeated opportunities to experience the same thing will build tolerance and perhaps even eventual acceptance. It is often thought that barefoot walks and sensory exploration is something limited to babies and toddlers, as they are tactile, sensory learners. Facilitating earthing with older children also has huge benefits for their overall development. The practice of forest bathing and mindfulness is perfect for older children, too, as it gives them the opportunity to slow down, listen to their body and appreciate the natural world. We know that being outside has a positive impact on mental health, and now more than ever, we need to provide our children with strategies to manage big emotions, something which is easier with older children who may have begun to have awareness of emotions.

Creating your outdoor space

So what does all this mean for early years settings and the creation of outdoor spaces that are conducive to creativity in young children. It is a good idea to take some time down at the child's level, observing your outdoor area from their perspective. Too often, we look at it through an adult's perspective – what we like and think looks good – but it is not us that the space is for, and it won't matter how fantastic the area looks if children are not engaging and using it to its full potential. Whether you have access to large grassed areas, concrete patches or artificial grass and mud, what matters isn't the size or shape but what you do with it.

Children need the opportunity to test their physical skills as they develop, so it's a good idea to have opportunities for them to climb, balance and swing if you can. Resources don't have to be expensive, and asking for donations of tyres, crates, pallets, boxes and tubes can be a great way to keep costs down and provide children with opportunities not only to climb but to build on a large scale and create their own structures.

Zoe Clark introduced large loose parts to her reception children in September to support not only their physical development but their imagination and ability to use narratives in their play.

We spent the first few weeks modelling potential play opportunities and soon, the children began to create their own. A group of 6 boys were making a rocket ship with the large loose parts which included crates, old console steering wheels and planks. The stacked the crates on either side, working collaboratively with little support. They later introduced planks and wheels into their design, proudly guarding against anyone wanting their steering wheels. They extended their play into the afternoon with role play, allowing a few pokemon characters to enter as well as iron man. At the end of the day they showed their design to their parents on pick up.

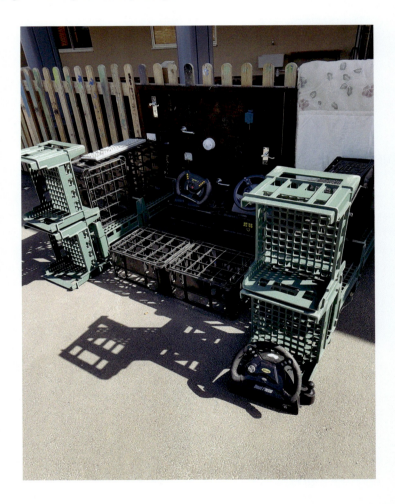

We can see from this example that at 4 years old, with mindful adults and a range of resources, children can develop their own narratives and extend their ideas without the need for expensive catalogue resources. It is easy to get caught up in Pinterest-worthy environments, but it is important to remember that these do not reflect your children and their lived experiences. The children who these environments were designed for are not your children, and they may not have the same interests or developmental needs. Children need you to understand their development to ensure they are appropriately challenged.

If you have a small space, the use of mirrors can make them look much bigger, and children will enjoy seeing their reflections, as well as noticing the trees, clouds and other elements of nature. Children benefit from a range of opportunities outdoors, and it is our role to make sure that they are available in order for children to develop their skills in perception, strength, large muscle movement and collaboration with others.

Many settings now have mud or texture kitchens outdoors for children to freely explore and use sand, mud, natural loose parts, flowers and herbs. Having a place for children to plant seeds is also supportive of children's understanding of growth and caring for living things. For those with larger areas, creating nooks and making resources available for den-building allows children to create their own spaces. This is as simple as using fabrics and pegs, and asking parents for donations of duvet covers and large fabrics can again be a way to keep costs down.

Reflecting on your children's interest can also provide inspiration for creating areas outside. Alongside providing high-quality continuous provision, loose parts and items that are familiar to the children, invitations to play and explore can also be set up in line with their current interests.

Opportunities to make marks outdoors and create, drawing inspiration from the environment is another great way for children to connect with nature.

Recycled and unwanted items such as sinks and baths can provide a great starting point for small worlds, fairy gardens or a vegetable garden by simply filing them with soil; of course, it is important you risk assess any recycled or donated items and ensure they are safe for the children. Creating sensory paths or play type specific areas

can also appeal to some provision where space is large enough to allow. It is worth carrying out regular audits of your outdoor environment to ensure it is still meeting the needs of the children and allows for reflection and change if needed.

The outdoors is exactly that – it is a space free of constraints and should be viewed as such. Practitioners need to remember that whilst bringing resources into our outdoor play spaces is something that can be done mindfully, there is a world outside that children can experience with little or no resources. Simply exploring the elements of wind, rain, wet grass and uneven terrain support sensory learning and exploration in children of all ages.

TOP TIPS FOR RECONNECTING WITH NATURE – LAURA BROTHWELL

1 Experience the weather (don't just describe it or name it, experience it through the senses).

2 Experience the effects of the changing seasons, not just the weather change but the changes within the environment or wildlife (leaves and blossom or migration or hibernation etc.).

3 Turn over a small allotment plot or add plant pots to your outdoor area or on window ledges.

4 Plant herbs – remember they are a perennial plant, so the more you harvest, the more they will grow – or fruit/vegetable plants, such as tomato or green beans, as they are easy to grow and abundant in harvest.

5 Turn off indoor artificial light and experience the tone and glow of natural light, noticing refraction and shadows.

6   Encourage wildlife to your area by hanging bird feeders or creating a bug hotel or a small water rockery.

7   Make the most of insect visitors; slow down and make time to connect, ponder and value the presence of any special visitors regardless of if it is a passing butterfly, spider in the corner of a room or bird flying overhead.

8   Involve families at home in small gardening projects, sharing seeds or taking part in outdoor adventures, collecting nature treasures to bring into provision to stock up on natural loose parts for creative play, storytelling and exploration.

9   Plan a time to adventure beyond your provision boundaries to explore the landscapes within your local community.

10 Value your own body and emotions as part of nature; practise gratitude, mindfulness, breathwork, meditation, yoga or tai chi.

Part 2

9 Let them play: Provocations

In the second part of the book, I will share what I believe are some invitations to play and create that not only are lots of fun for children but support their overall development. In this brief chapter, we will look closer at the notion of process art and valuing process over product when working with young children. We will also look at the elements of high-quality invitations to play that allow children to develop their creativity and how this impacts how they respond when given the time and space they need to create. In doing so, we will look at the difference between a provocation and an invitation to play and how these can support young children in their creative ideas and development of creative thinking.

Process over product

Process art is the most important way for children to enjoy art-making alongside their peers and adults, and even more so as children develop through their pre-school years since opportunities to explore are often replaced with more formal approaches to learning phonics and numbers. The focus of process art is exactly what it says in the title, the process. Practitioners engaging in this type of art-making with young children have no preconceived idea about how the invitation will

DOI: 10.4324/9781003271710-12

develop or how the children will engage with it. The beauty is in the magic that happens when children are given complete freedom over what and how to engage with a particular set of resources. Children can also often choose to return to a process art invitation as it is never completely finished; 'inside each wonder-based art project is an underlying process that captures the child's interest, and that interest fulfils a deep desire to experiment, invent and create' (Haughey, 2020:18).

There is no right or wrong with process art, something that many practitioners can find extremely difficult. Too often, those who work with young children, although with good intentions, try to direct or alter a child's thinking and ideas to suit their adult perceptions. Asking a child of 2 or 3 not to use all the glue or to only use the circle ones not only is unobtainable for a young child whose only desire is to create but also threatens their sense of autonomy. This is detrimental not only to their development but to their sense of self.

Imagine a child creating a self-portrait and painting their hair blue. Let's consider first the potential adult response:

- Is that what colour your hair is? I don't think it is?

- Here's the brown, I think you need brown for your hair.

- Oh dear, that doesn't look like you, does it?

Sound familiar? If this sounds like something you have ever said to a child, who, in your opinion, painted their hair the 'wrong' colour or their eyes in shades of bright pink, then I am grateful that you have read this far. That you are willing to reconsider the impact of allowing your perception to overtake that of the child's. Children express themselves in a range of ways, and we know that the more freedom they have to explore, the more developed their sense of themselves becomes. The belief that they are strong, are capable and have the ability to make their own choices is important for the development of creativity, and sometimes, practitioners can inadvertently stifle this. In the example of the self-portrait, stop and consider why the child may have chosen those colours and reflect on how you can reframe your language to affirm their decisions and remove your perception of how it should look. Comment and ask questions using the 'I wonder' framework. This will enable children to think about what they are doing and why without questioning if they are right. Instead of 'Is that what colour your hair is?', try 'I wonder what colour you're going to use for your hair?'. This ensures that the child feels empowered to choose what colour they'd like but also to think about that choice. There are no mistakes to be fixed in process art, and no two pieces look the same.

Conveyor craft or process art

> The way you would draw a tree is different from the way anyone else would draw a tree – and that's the way it's supposed to be!
>
> (Fred Rogers)

I have already touched on what it is to offer process art to young children. If you already offer a range of process art opportunities to the children in your care, then thank you. Thank you for advocating for young children and their right to choose and create what they like, what they are interested in and what fascinates them. Process art gives children the chance to explore different media and materials and choose their own ways to do things in a staged process where they can explore, create and then come up with their own innovative ideas about what to do next or how to extend their project.

This is a direct contrast to what I like to call a conveyor craft mentality. This type of offering is usually devoid of thinking about the child's capabilities or interests and instead is often used as a way to manage children. A practitioner dutifully cuts out penguin templates and offers the children only white and black paint. Every child in the room must carry out the activity, and at the end of the day, every child has the same black-and-white penguin. Although the brush strokes may be different, they will be the same size and shape, they will look the same (for the most part) and there is a definite end. Therefore, very little process involved. If this sounds like you, it may be time to reflect on why you offer experiences in this way, what benefit it serves and who you are doing it for. Management? Ofsted? Parents? It certainly isn't the children. If children have an interest, it is important they have every opportunity to explore it. If penguins and Antarctic animals is a fascination of your children, why not use photographs of the animals to encourage language. Offer them alongside black and white paint and let the children draw and represent their own. With photographs and books alongside these opportunities, children will have a real chance to see and understand what penguins look like. If you have small-world animals, these can be used as objects of reference, too.

As children get older, we need to provide opportunities to explore and investigate the world with purpose. Observational drawing can be great for this as children will use what they see to create representations. At Wally's, we provide provocations based on the children's interests to engage them in conversation and extend their thinking. In autumn, we offer pumpkins and squashes for drawing or painting, and in spring, use flowers in vases to spark thinking. We provide tools and resources to facilitate mark-making if they choose to. This is still within the realms of process art as the outcome is of little importance, and every image will look different according to the child's abilities. I know some will argue it is not true process art, and that's okay, too. What is important is that we understand why we are doing something, and if we have the child in the centre of that, we can't go wrong.

Provocations vs. invitations

The resources we have within our early years setting mean very little unless the children engage with them. We all know the saying that less is more, and this can certainly be the case when working in early years. As practitioners, it is our role to reflect on what we offer to the children on a daily basis and work with management and leadership teams to ensure we have high-quality resources available that reflect the developmental needs and the interests of the children. Part of our role, then, is also to present the resources we have in a way that excites children. We have discussed the need for resources to be accessible to children and for those who use in-the-moment planning, setting up the environment and continuous provision may be all that is needed.

Many settings now prefer to call the activities they set up for the children invitations. Invitations to play, invitations to learn, invitations to explore. In the general sense of the term, an invitation is given when we want to invite someone to do something, usually a party or perhaps a play date in the park. In terms of early years children, it is the same principle. That resources are arranged in such a way that children are invited to explore and play through meaningful invitations. These are usually set up based on the children's interests or something they have been observed playing with. It may be as simple as providing paint and paper alongside a vase of flowers to invite children to paint, or it can include some of their favourite things alongside mark-making resources, small figures, sensory elements and anything else that will excite the children's interest.

Provocations, in contrast, can be said to be all around us. 'Put simply, provocations provoke. This includes all aspects of learning and development, provoking interest, curiosity, discussion and discovery. They also provoke children's questions, queries, thoughts and ideas' (Longstaffe, 2020:15). There has been some concern that setting up provocations for children are, in fact, an extension of adult-led activities; however, the role of the adult in a provocation is to 'recognise the interests of the children, plan and set up a particular provocation and then to observe as the children explore, discover and interact with the resources' (Longstaffe, 2020:17). The main difference between this and an adult-led activity is that the children are in charge. They are free to engage with the provocation (or not) and have ownership over the experience, deciding what to do, how and for how long. In an adult-led activity, it is the adult who leads and directs the children to a particular outcome, something which is not the case for provocational learning and opportunities. Hayley Dyke, owner of Little Wise Owls Childminding, ensures that her children are offered opportunities to think independently and creatively through mindful provocations that she sets up regularly.

The role of the adult

The role of the adult is vital when considering how we can support young children to create. We have discussed this at length in Chapter 5 but feel that it is an important point to reiterate as we move towards the invitations to play in Part 2. The practitioners that care for young children need to ensure that they are role models and collaborators in children's play. By the age of 3, typically developing children possess enough language to be able to invite an adult into their play if they would like. For those children with special educational needs, those who are non-verbal or those who have delayed language and communication, their cues to adults will be in the form of eye contact and body language. It is important that staff are mindful of each child's needs and respond appropriately.

At Nina's Nursery High Lane, Amanda Redwood and her team know just how important it is for creative development that children have strong role models when exploring different media.

We believe that a settled child is a curious child, the relationships, and bonds that the staff form promote secure attachments that in turn promote confidence for the children to explore. The staff will model how to use different materials as they play alongside the children, another opportunity for time to bond and learn each other's interests as well as opportunities to scaffold learning. The staff are mindful to keep their interactions positive as children create and develop creatively, this helps avoid any sense of fear of judgement within the child's view of their own self or creations.

We know that the relationships we build with young children play a vital role in fostering creativity, and if children are to feel confident enough to explore, have the self-esteem to make mistakes and try again, and develop the skills they need for their future, then their interactions with adults have to be of the highest quality.

Igniting the senses

Art and play go hand in hand with the development of sensory exploration in young children. Children need to be provided with a multitude of resources and experiences to enhance their daily lives that tap into their senses and allow them to experience nature and their world in a multifaceted way. With the help of Laura Brothwell, founder of Stone Hen Childcare, we have collated a brief outline of the senses that can be ignited in young children and ways we can encourage children to use them.

Visual – landscapes/colour tone/patterns and shapes/wildlife/self-awareness/awe and wonder/seasonal change/weather/light and shadow/natural elements photography/ imagination/external awareness/inspiration

Supporting children's sense of the world through what they can see is crucial to their understanding.

■ Go for walks and comment on what you can see.

■ Describe features of the environment, such as animals or vehicles.

■ Engage in treasure hunts, looking for colours or patterns in nature.

■ Observe the weather and seasonal changes with young children, developing their vocabulary by extending their descriptions.

Auditory (sound) – soundscapes/onomatopoeia/weather/natural elements storytelling/ literature/music/poetry/song

Using what children tell you about what they hear can feed into many activities that support their auditory understanding.

■ Go for listening walks and encourage children to say what they hear.

■ Notice how different sounds are louder or quieter than others.

■ Play listening games using a variety of sounds (household/transport/animals).

■ Extend children's learning through listening to music or storytelling based on their interests.

Gustatory (taste) and olfactory (smell) – permaculture/baking/flowers/herbs/essential oils/natural elements/weather/foraging/harvesting baking/cooking and preparing meals/experimentation

The senses responsible for taste and smell are different for everyone. Whilst they work in the same way, how a child perceives a particular taste or smell may be completely different to their peers.

■ Encourage children to taste and smell a variety of foods to increase their willingness to try and develop a can-do attitude.

■ Grow herbs or vegetables in the garden to provide regular opportunities to care for the plants that can then be harvested and used in cooking.

■ Notice that children often like to taste the rain. We have all seen children look up at the sky whilst it is raining. Encourage these abstract ways of thinking in their early years so that children eventually learn they can try new things and think outside the norm to find solutions.

Tactile (touch) – textures/connection/vibration/natural elements/weather/transient art/ painting/design and construction/marks and symbols

Apart from their visual sense, a child's tactile experience will not only define the things they enjoy but allow them to form ideas about what they dislike, too.

- Provide rich sensory experiences for children to get involved in on a daily basis.

- Children need the opportunity experience things they don't like, too. With encouragement and modelling, children can enjoy a range of tactile experiences.

- Provide lots of resources that have different textures to explore, as it is great for language development, too.

Vestibular (balance) and proprioceptive (sense of space and movement) – climbing/crawling/yoga/force and flow of natural elements/den building/gardening/ grounding/yoga/tai chi/swings and hammocks/open space for gross motor expression sculpting/dance/movement/design and construction/architecture/innovation

Developing a child's sense of balance and space can be difficult if they are not used to confidently using climbing equipment, but there are plenty of other ways it can be supported.

- Introduce yoga or dance and movement sessions to calmly introduce concepts of balance.

- Allow lots of uninterrupted time outdoors to run, climb, crawl and move.

Interoceptive (internal) – mindfulness/meditation/breathwork/emotional intelligence/ daydreaming/visualisation/recalling memory/effects of weather and temperature upon our body/self-regulation/biological awareness/empathy/compassion/resilience/setting intentions/confidence/connection/free expression

Children need to feel calm, valued and listened to in order that their interoceptive sense is developed throughout childhood. This involves much more than tick box activities and requires mindful adults who understand the children and their needs.

- Have children start practising breathwork from 3 (children younger than 3 can try it, too, but it becomes more effective with pre-school-age children).

- Try starting the day with some hot chocolate breathing. This is great to set the tone, particularly as you never know how a child started their day. Ask the children to close their eyes; on the inhale, they pretend to smell their hot chocolate, and on the exhale, they gently blow it (as it's hot).

- Know that emotions are often high in this age group, so ready stories with meanings can embed empathy and understanding of simple emotions and perspectives.

- Provide opportunities for children to explore emotions, such as transient art invitations or mark-making.

Giving children time

Unplanned time can be the catalyst for creativity. More and more children are having their lives scheduled for them with endless extra-curricular activities, meaning there is less time for them to play. Having periods during the week where children do not have anything to do or anywhere to go leaves more free time for unplanned activities, and this is where parents and often practitioners begin to see behaviour they associate with boredom. Instead of embracing it, parents and practitioners are quick to fill children's time, offering suggestions or getting out arts and crafts to keep children busy. There are several problems with this; children quickly learn to be occupied by others. They are unable to play independently and rely on others to give them something to do. For children who attend early years settings, they present as having lower levels of self-confidence and are unable to manage times when they have freedom to choose their own activities. These children will look for reassurance from adults or ask questions such as, 'what are we doing now?'. They may also stand or sit, observing others but not directly engaging with their environment or their peers due to a lack of autonomy. Often, if they are not used to this level freedom, they are confused and unsure about what is expected of them. Slowing down, embracing the space and stepping out of the schedule allow ideas to be born.

Outdoor nature play

Nature can provide wonderful inspiration for children's creative explorations. It is a changing landscape that offers lots to explore, from playing with shadows, creating with natural loose parts or exploring and experimenting with sand, water and mud, some of which we will look at in detail over the following pages. Older children could draw, take photographs or collect some of the things they see, and this will inspire further explorations. Exploring the natural world is a wonderful way to promote problem-solving and imaginative play and develop the skills children need in order to thrive.

Loose parts

Loose parts, as we have seen, are simply collections of objects that can be moved and combined in a temporary way. Children use their imaginations to engage with everyday objects or items found in nature. There is no predetermined way of playing with them; instead, the possibilities of how they are used are open-ended and determined by the child, and it is here that real creative thinking exists. Encouraging leadership to allow small groups of children the chance to go on journeys to search and collect, choosing things that appeal to them, and from this, they can create a collection that is meaningful to them, but if it is not possible, there are things you can do. Instead, why not forage for items in your setting garden or ask children to bring in a bag of nature's treasures for use in the play space. For example, pebbles, sticks, buttons, blocks of wood, fabrics, lids and containers can all make great loose parts. It is important to risk assess any loose parts or found objects before allowing the children to interact with them.

Mark-making

Children often enjoy the sensory and physical aspects of mark-making, and it appeals to all children because it is open-ended. Younger children can express themselves in a range of ways when given pencils, crayons, paints and other early mark-making resources. As children get older, drawing is an opportunity for children to represent their thoughts and ideas. In this way, they can make their thoughts and ideas visible, which helps practitioners to understand and engage with their thinking and be able to offer invitations to play based on the emerging themes in their marks which you can talk about together. In her childminding practice, this is something that Martine Crowley actively encourages.

Exploring and investigating light and reflection

Many settings have begun to understand the importance of providing opportunities for children that provoke their thinking beyond the norm. A wonderful resource often not valued highly enough is light. Practitioners at Little Learners use light to enhance their play spaces, providing opportunities for children to become deeply absorbed in their investigations. They create textured small spaces where children can closely observe light and its many properties and use projectors to develop their environment and provoke creativity.

Nina's Nursery High Lane also place great value on the quality of their environment, and well-placed mirrors provide opportunities for children to see themselves and their activities reflected within them.

Light can be used in many ways to develop not only children's play but their deeper critical thinking and creativity. Light is a versatile resource that lends itself to investigation in terms of movement, shadows, how it is created and how it is produced. Reflections Small School encourage children to use light in innovative ways to extend children's knowledge and independent enquires.

Lights can also be introduced and used to support language and communication. Children at Reggio & Co love using puppets to recreate and act out narratives in their play.

Whether it's natural light shining in through windows, providing a warmth throughout the room, or light that has been purposefully placed to introduce new ideas or abstract ways of thinking, children often delight in the wonder that is provides.

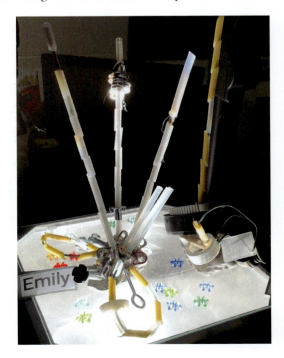

Are you ready?

I hope in this chapter I have given you an insight into what is to come throughout the last few chapters of this book. We have looked in detail at the senses and how these can be supported with young children on a daily basis in our practice. If you are already part of the process art movement, then you are already doing something great by supporting the next generation of creative thinkers. If you are leaning towards process art and open-ended experiences for the young children in your care but are not quite there yet, it is my hope I have given you cause for reflection and that you will be ready to have important conversations with colleagues about your values and ethos surrounding how to support children to develop their creative thinking and exploration.

10 Discover cooking with young children

Cooking with young children is unlike anything else in early years. Children are often motivated by food, but putting that aside, it provides so many opportunities to develop language, communication, mathematical concepts, collaboration with others and, above all, creativity since you never know how it will turn out. Whilst some might argue that since cooking usually follows a recipe and has a clear goal, it cannot be creative nor process-driven; however, I would tend to disagree since we have seen throughout this book that creativity has so many facets, and often, it is the process children find most enjoyable.

I have detailed here four easy-to-follow recipes for creating food with young children from the age of 2. It will, of course, be a matter of knowing your children to establish what you think they are ready for, and I have also given details if they can be adapted for different age groups. With any food-based activities, you will need to risk assess any child with

DOI: 10.4324/9781003271710-13

allergies and substitute ingredients where possible. Many of the recipes here can be adapted for those with dairy, gluten and egg allergies, and all are natural nut-free.

Following on from the cooking itself, for recipes that require it, children can also be encouraged to create envelopes to take home their cooking, or children can sit together and enjoy what they have made, creating a moment of connection between them. Practitioners can print the recipe for children to have a go at with their parents, too, another way to encourage home learning.

Ensure children wash their hands before and after preparing food, and long hair should be tied up. Children learn from role models, so make sure they see you washing your hands, tying back long hair and wearing an apron.

Invitations in the chapter include the following:

- 1, 2, 3 biscuits

- Perfect pizzas

- Rainbow salad

- Dandelion cookies

- Other ideas

1, 2, 3 biscuits

1, 2, 3 biscuits are a great way for children to start out in their independent cooking journey. Ideally, children will have some understanding of numbers up to 3 for them to know how much of each ingredient to use, but practitioners can support young children if they are not quite ready for this yet. Children will mix the ingredients with their hands, providing a hands-on learning experience, and will build their vocabulary, focussing on concepts and mathematical language.

How-to

1   Ask all the children to wash their hands and get an apron (if you have them).

2   Provide each with a small bowl.

3   Provide the group with a tub for each ingredient. For this recipe, you will need the following:

   a   Sugar

   b   Butter or margarine

   c   Flour

4   Place them in the middle of the table with tablespoons in each; you could also use any number resources to show the children how many of each they will need.

5   Promote turn-taking, early sharing and communication skills with children by explaining that they do not need their own spoon. Depending on the size of the group, you may wish to add one or two extra spoons to avoid waiting.

6   Have children prepare the following in their bowls;

   a   1 tablespoon of sugar

   b   2 tablespoons of butter

   c   3 tablespoons of flour

7   Ask them to start mixing them together with their fingers when they have all their ingredients in their bowl, to form a dough. Staff can be nearby to support children and encourage them to talk about what they are doing. If the dough isn't coming together, they will need more butter, and if it is too wet, a little more flour can be added.

8   Have children take it out of the bowl when it has formed into a dough and roll it onto a floured surface or board.

9   Note that this recipe is all about having minimal tools and promoting physical skills, so no rolling pins are required. Spin, spin, spin, pat, pat, pat, turn – then repeat. The dough will start to get bigger and flatten as children follow the steps.

10   Have them cut out shapes if you have cutters or place their circle biscuits on a baking tray for cooking.

11   Bake them for eight to ten minutes in the oven on a medium heat.

Top tips

■ Children do not need their own ingredient tubs. One tub of each big enough for around six to eight children is perfect.

■ This is a great sensory experience as children will use their hands to combine the ingredients into a dough; for children will sensory needs, they can, of course, use a spoon to mix their dough.

■ As children become more confident, they do not need direct supervision, but practitioners should be on hand for support if children need it.

■ As always, children benefit from a good role model, so why not make a biscuit yourself. Add ingredients into your own bowl and talk about what you are doing; this will encourage children to think critically about what is in their own bowls.

■ A great variation for younger children if you are not confident in their ability to form a dough on their own is to allow them to mix ingredients together freely; this will allow them the chance to explore the ingredients and amounts on their own. If they are too young to understand the need to count out the spoons, practitioners can hand-make a dough, making enough for everyone, and when the children have finished with their concoctions, staff can hand them a ball of dough to manipulate and shape into their biscuit.

Perfect pizza

This is such an easy recipe and is suitable for all children to take part independently. Of course, I will always advocate for making a simple pizza base with the children first (recipe as follows), or you can buy one readymade for them to add their ingredients onto if you would prefer.

How-to

For the pizza base, you will need the following:

1   500g plain flour

2   ½ teaspoon dried yeast

3   400ml warm water

4   Oil/butter or greaseproof paper to ensure your base doesn't stick to the baking tray

A note on proving – usually, you need to prove recipes that contain yeast for a number of hours before shaping and cooking. This can be time-consuming when working with children but should be done if you can. You will need to decide whether you have time to prove your dough; in all the recipes I have used with children, if we have time to spare, we will. If we don't, I won't. Children don't need perfect.

Combine the dry ingredients first and then slowly add the warm water to make a dough. Knead and roll into circles.

You can then prepare toppings. Again, this should be done with the children where possible as they can; with supervision, chop vegetables, such as tomatoes, mushrooms and peppers.

Keeping in mind allergies and food preferences, you could also provide ham, cheese, pineapple and pepperoni, along with any other ingredients the children would like. A great way to keep portion size and waste to a minimum is to use a muffin tray for the toppings; this way, children can select what they want to add, and you don't end up chopping vegetables you don't need.

Top tips

■ Ensure the children use a tomato sauce base as glue to stick their ingredients on. Mathematical language should be used to extend and further their knowledge about whether they have enough or not and how much of what ingredients they'd like to use.

■ Put a little extra cheese on top to make sure the ingredients stay where they were put.

■ Pop them on a medium heat until the cheese has melted, as pizzas are quick to cook.

Snail salad (edible for humans)

Using fresh ingredients in cooking is always a great way to encourage conversation around healthy eating and oral health. Children often associate baking with biscuits

and cakes, as this is what many parents will tend to bake at home. There are those children who may have never cooked before; using tools may be an alien concept, and they may have little or no knowledge of ingredients and how they can be used. It is our role to introduce the ideas and creativity of cooking gradually, introducing concepts and utensils and staying present and in the moment with them.

One of the children at Wally's pre-school got an African land snail for her birthday. This led to discussions about where they live, how they move and what they eat. Cue a trip to the local supermarket to prepare a feast for her new pet. You can use a variety of fresh vegetables; for our snail salad, we used technology to our advantage and researched vegetables land snails eat. We used the following:

- Apples

- Tomatoes

- Cucumber

- Celery

- Strawberries

The children showed high levels of engagement as they peeled, chopped, felt and described what they were doing. We had a tasting session at the end, and the group were so excited to be able to take their finished salads home.

Using nature's ingredients: Dandelion cookies

Children love to cook and have a sense of achievement when they have something to show for their efforts. Allowing children the opportunity to forage for ingredients when outdoors gives them ownership of their recipe, and using what they find to extend their cooking repertoire is great to build on their knowledge and understanding of how we can use what nature gives us.

For this easy collaborative recipe, you will need the following:

- ½ cup oil

- ½ cup honey

- 2 eggs

- 1 teaspoon vanilla extract

- 1 cup flour

- 1 cup oats

- ½ cup dandelion flowers

There are two ways of working when carrying out group opportunities.

The first is to have a small group gathered with an adult who is able to read and guide them to follow the instructions. This works well as the adult can support the children in weighing the ingredients and ensuring that they all get a turn to participate.

The second way is by dividing the group into two. Ingredients are pre-weighed and placed on a third table, and the adult has more of a supervisory role, encouraging listening, attention and teamwork. In this role, the practitioner reads the instructions clearly, and each group must work together to get their recipe ready to be cooked.

You will need to make a decision as to which method you prefer to use; I often jump between the two depending on what the objective was. If it was to support listening skills, then I will use the teamwork method as it matters less that the ingredients haven't been weighed by the children, and this method encourages children to use their critical thinking and problem-solving. If the practitioners don't explicitly say, 'you'll need a bowl', the children have to think about where they will put their ingredients before they start and subsequently find a bowl. If the objective was to introduce mathematical concepts, support children's independence or spend time with the group; it would be the whole-group method.

How-to

You'll need to let the children help you prepare the flowers they've picked.

- Ensure they are washed thoroughly.

- Measure the required quantity of intact flowers into a cup.

- Hold the flowers upside down and pinch the green base; this will release the yellow part – now, they are ready.

Don't worry if there is any green remaining – all parts of a dandelion are edible.
The following is for the biscuit dough:

- Add oil and honey to the bowl – mix.

- Crack the eggs into the bowl – mix.

- Stir in the flour, oats and flowers.

- Drop the batter onto a baking tray (greased).

- Bake for ten to fifteen minutes on a medium heat.

Other ideas

I have also provided a short list of other easy-to-prepare and easy-to-make recipes for young children. They provide opportunities for development across all the areas of learning as well as the chance to spend time connecting with their peers and key people.

Painted toast

This is great for toddlers and pre-school children alike. Simply mix a few food colourings of choice with either milk or natural yoghurt, and the children can paint a slice of bread. Children can show their creative designs, and once finished, practitioners can toast them for the children to enjoy.

Soups

Soups are a fantastic way to promote physical skills and support language. Children can peel, chop, dice and cut a range of vegetables before adding them to the pan to boil and then blend.

If you can, making fresh bread rolls is a perfect accompaniment. Since the objective with soup is usually in the preparation, a shop-bought bread mix will provide a quick roll that will be ready in time for lunch; of course, you can make them from scratch, too. Perfect for enjoying in the woods or after a busy morning playing.

Pea muffins

Cooking with young children is a really easy way to get them talking about their likes and dislikes and encourage them to try new foods. You can also find stories to inspire your bakes. Reading a story first will build anticipation of what they might make and encourage language as they may guess the ingredients.

Biscuit additions

Using the 1, 2, 3 method as a base, children can add a range of flavourful ingredients. Why not take advantage of what nature has to offer. You could gather blackberries for blackberry biscuits or forget-me-nots for a beautiful floral tone.

When foraging, please make sure you follow some basic rules:

1   Only collect from areas that have not been contaminated with pesticides.

2   Only collect what you know is edible. If you are unsure, its best to leave it.

3   Only collect what you are allowed – it is illegal to pick certain flowers in public areas. Make sure you do your research to ensure you can safely manage foraging for cooking.

Stir-fry vegetables

I absolutely love our induction hob at pre-school. It is so easy to use; just plug it in and pop the pan on. It can be used to make fritters, make pancakes, cook vegetables and much, much more. They are safe to use as they do not get too hot, and when the pan is removed, the heat is forced to stop generating.

Of course, you must risk assess having a hob accessible to children, but the benefits for them to see something change in the pan before their eyes are second to none. Chop up some of their favourite vegetables and toss them in a wok with a little soy sauce. These serve as a great accompaniment to a noodle or rice dish for lunch.

Pancakes

Pancakes are really easy for the children to mix up themselves, and they can't go wrong with the ingredients. One egg, some flour and a little milk all mixed up in a bowl or jug. Working alongside professionals is a great

opportunity to see how things are made and create the idea of role models. Every so often, why not invite one or two children to prepare food alongside your chef. Children will gain not only further knowledge of important techniques, like how to crack an egg, but they will also gain confidence, too.

Bread shapes

Children love to reflect their interests in their play, and what better way to combine a love of cooking and animals than creating some of our favourites using bread. Since the overall aim of the session is to manipulate and shape the bread, packet bread mix will work just as well and ensures that the children have enough time to shape and prove their bread before baking. Providing an object of reference or books will give the children a guide as to what their bread should look like. In the example, children used bread dough to create frogs using small-world animals and books for reference.

Discover communication and language

Language and literacy are cultivated through ongoing storytelling and quality interaction with the practitioners who support and develop children's ideas and inquiry, creative thinking and collaboration with others. We fully value that children communicate their thoughts, emotions and ideas through creative expression, thus allowing us to tailor a proactive approach to observe, sustain and scaffold children's learning throughout the creative process.

Communication and language are vital skills for children to succeed not only in their early years but into adolescence and their adult lives, and the foundations start from birth. The way we interact and talk to children about what they are doing, how they feel and what they need forms the crucial bonds that are so important in their development. Everything we do with children provides opportunities to develop their communication skills; however, those experiences that provide a sensory element are fantastic for building vocabulary and building confidence along the way. They are also accessible to all children, regardless of their communicative ability or educational need, as they are open-ended, process-based opportunities.

Invitations in the chapter include the following:

- Puffy paint

- Story dough

- Clay explorations

- Alcohol ink mugs and gifts

- Sharing stories and bookish play

- Layering

DOI: 10.4324/9781003271710-14

Puffy paint

I love puffy paint. If you have never used it before, please promise you'll give it a try after reading. This puffy paint can be made up ahead of time or done with the children. It is not the same as shaving foam and food colouring; the effect is different, and this recipe has to be cooked for its beauty to be truly appreciated. As with all process art, there is no preconceived idea about how it will turn out. Children can use as much as they like, the more the better, as it will puff right up once it has been cooked. The magic doesn't have to stop there either. Children can add to their creations using felt pens, crayons, gems and other treasures.

To make puffy paint, you will need the following:

- Flour

- Salt

- Baking powder (optional – gives it a little more puff)

- Water

- Food colouring

How-to

- Add together the ingredients in a muffin or cake tin, one for each colour:

  - 1 tablespoon flour

  - 1 tablespoon salt

  - 1 teaspoon baking powder

  - 2 tablespoons water

  - 5 drops of food colouring

- Note that this will make one colour.

- Repeat for all six or twelve colours.

- Encourage the children to get some paper and a paintbrush, and they can begin painting.

- Allow them to freely create anything they choose; using more paint will create a puffier picture.

- Have staff (with the children's help, if possible) microwave their picture for thirty seconds, when they have finished.

- Watch as it instantly dries and gets puffy.

Top tips

- Provide children with other resources that they can add to their picture when it is dry.

- Know that this is great for younger children, as the microwave means it is instantly dry.

- Encourage communication by talking to the children about the changes that are happening as they paint and then as it dries.

Story dough

We all love play dough, whether it is for sensory play or fine motor skill development, or made by adults or the children. I bet we all know an early years practitioner who has perfected the art of a good dough.

So what can we do with it once it's been made? There are so many options, it's hard to list them all, but one quite fascinating way to keep children focussed with high levels of engagement is to use it alongside

stories. We will look at other bookish play ideas a little later, but introducing dough and other props alongside children's favourite books allows them to think creatively and use the story as a guide in extending their own play. Mindful practitioners can also sit close by and observe the play, waiting to be invited in or adding comments to support the children's language development.

How-to

- Make up play dough in a variety of colours; this will be influenced by the book you choose. In this example of *The Tiger Who Came to Tea*, children were invited to use orange and red dough.

- Keep with the story by having practitioners add a small ceramic tea set featuring cups, saucers and a wooden birthday cake.

- Have other additions, including a spice mix (for added texture) and coloured pasta in several shapes (it is a tea party after all).

- We have some fantastic story spoons for *The Tiger Who Came to Tea*, so these were also added, of course, alongside the story.

Top tips

- Stand back – this is so important when working with young children. They do not need you to interfere.

- Know that children are capable of leading their own play when they have the chance. You will know your children and their developmental needs; if they need support from a familiar adult, be there, but the real magic happens when it comes from the child.

Clay explorations

Malleable materials are materials that children can shape themselves by pulling, stretching, pushing, rolling, squeezing, poking or pinching. Play dough or clay is great for this. You could make your own play dough and combine this with twigs, straws, stones, lids or feathers. Simple tools from around the house can be introduced alongside the malleable materials, developing children's coordination and agility. You could also use items such as garlic presses, pastry rollers and spoons.

Top tips

■ Offer children a lump of clay.

■ Provide water in spray bottles for them to use as they need and allow ample time to explore the texture of the clay.

■ Offer children additional resources such as petals, lentils, beans and other small loose parts they can push and add to their creations.

■ Know that some children are happy exploring the dough independently, but others may need some support. Be nearby so that you can provide encouragement if it is needed.

■ Take this as a great opportunity to learn language associated with sensory input. Children can learn to describe the texture, the temperature and how it changes when it has been manipulated by tools or hands.

■ Note that older children may start to represent their ideas through this media. Adults can support this stage of development by introducing technique to children, including how to use particular clay tools or how the water should be applied.

Alcohol ink mugs – inspired by love of learning childcare

Those of us who subscribe to the process art way of creating with young children are always on the lookout for new and innovative ways to stay true to the nature of process art, away from the conveyor craft mentality of creating twenty identical Mother's Day cards, but also allow the children to create something they are proud of to gift to a loved one.

For this opportunity, you will need the following:

- A white ceramic mug (each child will need their own)

- Alcohol inks

- Straws

- Rubbing alcohol

- Epoxy resin

How-to

- Have the children take their mug and choose the colours they'd like to use.

- Drip the ink (one by one) onto the mug.

- Offer straws in case any of the children want to blow the ink; they can also lift up the mug and move it, watching as the ink moves. Alternatively, it can be left to drip.

- Have them choose to add a drop of rubbing alcohol here and there; this will help the ink to spread and create beautiful patterns – no two will be the same.

- Have the adult cover it with equal parts epoxy and resin once the mug has dried, leaving it to dry for several days before presenting it.

Top tips

- The staff must ensure the children wash their hands after they have finished their mug.

- Other ceramic items can be used too, such as coasters or placemats.

- Children can be offered pipettes to ensure only small amounts of ink and rubbing alcohol is available.

- This activity must be supervised at all times, and I would suggest considering the age and developmental stage of your children before carrying it out.

- All hazardous liquids should be stored out of reach and put back when not in use.

Sharing stories and bookish play ideas

Sharing stories together often sparks the imagination. Stories can be explored in an active way through play and costume. The way we present our resources to children will have a huge impact on the way they access them independently and the way they engage with them.

Claire Wilson has a home-based provision where she takes steps to encourage children to access books independently and ensure they have a range of authentic resources and props available to them to support their play and storytelling.

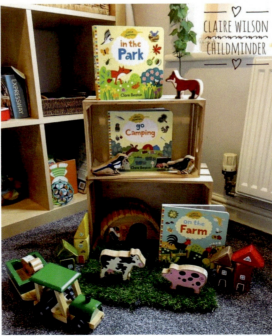

Top tips

■ Arrange props alongside books so that children can see clearly what is available to them.

■ Rotate stories so that children have exposure to a range of tales and supporting resources.

■ Create small spaces where children can go to sit and read together.

- Encourage children who speak English as an additional language to point and copy your words to build vocabulary around familiar words and objects.

- Set up invitations to explore the children's favourite books.

  - Having a tea party alongside the story of *The Tiger Who Came to Tea*

  - Peeling and chopping potatoes to make chips for the story of *The Best Chip*

  - Recreating the dinner scene using cooked spaghetti and gathering the bears around the table to re-enact the story *Teddy Bears Moving Day*

Layering – inspired by Reggio & Co

The key to understanding layering is not to overcomplicate it. It is simply using resources to form a layered effect. Borne out of an interest in the earth's layers, staff at Reggio & Co provided photographs and books to demonstrate how the layers look from the crust down to the core. They used transparent cubes to invite the children to layer with different resources.

How-to

- Give each child their own box.

- It should be clear so that the layers can be clearly seen.

- Provide a range of materials for the children to use alongside photographs of different things that have a layered effect or pattern.

- Provide, for example, a layered ice cream sundae, a sand art ornament or photographs and books that look at stripes and patterns.

- Invite the children to fill their box in a layered fashion.

PREK2 got to work on their rendition of Earth's layers. Pushing and shoving and pouring and placing tiny loose parts to create the most beautiful masterpieces. We used to believe that art work should come off the paper sometimes. Now? We are convinced art might have to be this 3D all the time.

(Candace Schoolman, Reggio & Co)

Inspired by what she had seen, Lexis Heal, who works in a homeschool co-op, was inspired to create a layered art piece with her group, shown here alongside photographs of layered effects.

12 Discover physical

Physical development is the cornerstone of being able to do things independently and having the confidence to do so and ask for help if they need it. Without strong muscles, children can find some of the most basis physical tasks a challenge, and this is becoming more apparent in our early years settings. Children find it difficult to hold themselves up on climbing frames due to reduce movement within the home and an increase in the use of electronic devices. Something that is also having a huge impact on children's developing skills is parents who have kept their children in a safety net, not allowing them to engage in what can be considered risk and adventure play, and when children have had the chance, they're told to be careful or don't jump, run, bounce. How can we expect children to develop their skills when they are constantly being reminded to be careful. This sends a strong message that we don't trust them, something that could potentially lead to low self-esteem and a lack of a can–do attitude.

In this chapter, I will share some of my favourite ideas to engage children, some that produce beautiful pieces but still keeping the process at the heart.

Invitations in the chapter include the following:

- Hapa Zome

- Drill painting

- Bits 'n' bobs masterpieces

- Painting

    - At height

    - Vertically

    - From below

- Mixed-media creations

DOI: 10.4324/9781003271710-15

Hapa Zome

For those who don't know, Hapa Zome, also known as flower bashing, is a great way to strengthen muscles, make beautiful artwork and aid children's gross motor skills. It is an art form originating in Japan and involves smashing flowers into fabrics, creating a print. Children can use rocks or hammers to smash their chosen flowers and can marvel at the print left behind. As with most process art ideas, there is no preconceived idea as to how it will turn out. This also means that beyond a small list of resources you may need to gather, the how-to is simple.

How-to

- Give children, a piece of fabric to sandwich their flowers. A rectangular piece will allow the children to add their flowers to the fabric and fold it over making a square.

- Have children collect their own flowers on a walk around the setting or local park, or you could provide vibrant bouquets for them.

- Place scissors near vases of flowers to encourage the children to chop the flower head or petals they want for an added element of independence.

- Encourage them to arrange their flowers on the fabric; the more colours the better.

- Fold over the fabric, completely covering the flowers.

- Bash – using the rock or hammer, simply bash the petals repeatedly until you start to see the colours bleed onto the fabric. That means it's working.

Top tips

- Children can also use paper if you don't have fabric; this can produce vibrant colours as the paper does not absorb the colour from the petal; however, the pattern is not as impressive as when using fabric.

- Children can use hammers or rocks. It is entirely dependent on what you have available, and both support physical skills in different ways. Whilst a rock develops strength and grasp in hand muscles, hammers explore force and speed as children have to bring them up and bang them down repeatedly.

- You can add sticks when it is finished to create a beautiful frame for your artwork, or you can make a hanging by adding sticks to the bottom and the top of the fabric.

Drill painting – inspired by Child First Moulton

We believe in the importance of children having the opportunity to become fully immersed in their creative side. Tactile experiences offer so much more than the traditional 2-dimensional art activities normally offered to children.

(Angela Green, Manager)

Young children are by nature curious about the world around them and often want to imitate others. This activity, inspired by Child First Moulton brings real-life working tools into art-making. As with Hapa Zome earlier, children have the opportunity to work firsthand with tools under the watchful supervision of mindful practitioners, developing strength and muscle tone alongside creating beautiful, original artwork.

How-to

Activities such as this, with a little thought, require very little setup. As mentioned, brushes can be pre-loaded and ready inside the drills for the children.

Top tips

- Drills can be preloaded with paintbrushes for younger children from the age of around 2.

- Pre-school children may be able to help load them and choose the thickness of the brushes they want to use.

- It is a good idea to talk about safety elements with the children either before they begin or whilst doing it. Practitioners can integrate safety messages through commenting on the speed of the drill or how it moves.

It is important to risk assess, ensure that any wires are kept safely and hazards are minimised.

Further ideas

Why not try adding card to the end of the drill and watching it spin. This fantastic variation, inspired by Sheila Lucas, Atelierista at Dolce Daycare & Pre-School, allows children to watch how the tools work and observe the concept of speed and shape. Simply attach the card to the drill and allow the children to use a variety of colours to create their patterns.

Bits 'n' bobs masterpieces

Children love to create, and these bits 'n' bob masterpieces provide the perfect way for children to choose their own resources with no pre-conceived ideas from practitioners. There is no intended outcome and nothing pre-planned, other than perhaps collecting odd and interesting bits for them to use.

How-to

■ Provide each child with a base. We found wooden offcuts from some nursery dividers we no longer needed. It doesn't matter what you use as long as you make sure it provides a big enough surface area for the child to build on and is strong enough to stand the weight, especially if using wooden loose parts and other heavier objects.

- Ask the children to get a pot for their glue (you could encourage them to have one between two children for early turn-taking and sharing) and a glue spreader.

- Ensure everything that is available to use is within easy reach (don't mistake this for getting everything for them; children should be able to find their own resources in the environment), and that's it.

Top tips

Children will love creating these masterpieces. Each one will be unique to the child and reflect what they are interested in. Some children will build up to form towers or bridges, and others will build out, creating perhaps rivers or roads.

- Be mindful not to ask children what they are making. They may not know, and for children who find free choice difficult, it may alter their thinking and revert them back to asking what to make and what they should use.

- Invite the children to paint their creation, once dry, using either water-based paint mixed with PVA (to stop cracking) or acrylic.

Painting

Painting is a great way for children to express themselves. Beyond the obvious benefit of creating beautiful artwork that can be kept or sent home to parents, it gives children the opportunity to explore their senses, what it feels like to touch it, what it can smell like and how they can manipulate it using tools. Toddlers love to body paint, and practitioners should allow this. Using their hands to cover their arms, legs and body in paint is a way for them to experience sensory input, how it feels on their skin, how it smears, how it may be cold and slippery. Older children should be given this opportunity, too, if they initiate it. It is part of our role to share different perspectives and pose questions to extend their learning. Painting on a horizontal surface is great, but how can we use our knowledge of children to facilitate what they need at this age and encourage them to move their bodies and develop control and strength.

We can draw on what we know about young children's physical skills by providing opportunities to paint at different heights, on different surfaces and with other parts of our bodies to challenge the children's thinking about what it means to paint.

How-to

There is minimal how-to for experiences where the children are in charge. It can be as simple as proving a ladder in your environment or as elaborate as wrapping every available surface in clingfilm for the children to paint freely. Often, with larger projects, it is better to be outside; however, with enough clear preparation, it can be manageable indoors, too.

- Using step ladders for younger children to reach gives them another perspective on which to form new ideas.

- Using plastic wrap around trees or poles gives children the chance to see their friends whilst they create.

- Draping fabrics over the top of the children and securing them will develop their physical skills as they reach above them to make marks.

- Hanging paper fans or large sheets of lace is a great way to develop children's co-ordination as they notice how it moves as they touch it with the brush.

Top tips

- Provide children with enough paint to explore freely without running out. If you are on a budget, then using bottles and adding a little water can make a little paint go a long way.

- Have water available for children to wash their hands (and feet) if they need to following the activity.

- Ensure you have somewhere you can leave their artwork to dry as trying to negotiate a large piece of painted plastic or fabric can be tricky.

Mixed-media creations – inspired by Reggio & Co and Jaci Pastrana

The best way for creativity to flourish is to provide children with time to process their ideas and the freedom to carry them out. Mixed-media creations are exactly that. They utilise lost, broken and no longer needed resources as well as those items that children find and use as their treasures. The priority in art-making like this is that children have the autonomy to decide what they create and even revisit it several times before coming to the conclusion that they are finished.

They appear similar to bits and bobs masterpieces, but the emphasis is on scale. Mixed-media creations are generally smaller and 2D with a slight height whereas the resources used for bits and bobs masterpieces are usually larger bricks, plastic toys and wooden offcuts.

How-to

- Collect a range of interesting resources in the centre of a large table.

- Ensure the children have enough glue (PVA is best) and something to spread it with.

- Ask each child to find a base (or if you had something in mind, you could lay out the number you need ready for the children to claim a station).

- Add paint to the table for added layering.

- Let them create.

In her invitation, Jaci Pastrana offered broken crayons and those not needed to create a mixed-media piece. She writes this:

> I offered a broken crayon, he automatically pinched the crayon with his index finger and thumb, resembling that sought after tripod grasp. We went through our whole bucket of crayons and broke them into half or even thirds. Then we peeled the paper off the crayons, which is an excellent fine motor exercise as well. Naturally, we had to repurpose the crayon label scraps and glue them down onto a painted canvas.

Top tips

- Please make sure you risk assess any broken resources before offering them to the children. Despite the beauty they may create, if they are not safe, they must be thrown away.

- Start collecting ahead of the project. That way, you will have enough if a child decides to initiate a collage.

- Ask parents for donations from home of old pencils, crayons, CDs, coins or other items they no longer need. Of course, these will need to be risk assessed, too.

- Offer different options for connecting and adding resources, depending on the age of the children. Glue guns can be provided an instant stick, and Sellotape will add another dimension to their art.

13 Discover outdoors

It is my hope that throughout this book, I have provided a wealth of information and inspiration for getting children into the outdoors. We know how important it is that young children experience the world through all their senses, and there is nowhere that has more sensory benefits than in nature. With the freedom to move their bodies, breathe in fresh air and take in the sounds and sights, children don't need a huge range of toys or resources to enjoy the outdoors; found and collected objects can provide a great basis for fantastic play.

In this chapter, I will share some of my favourite ideas to engage children outside; some even include no prep time and no resources, so there really can be no excuse for not giving them a try. Invitations in the chapter include the following:

- Puddle patterns

- Collections in nature

- Large-scale painting

- Potion water play

- Marvellous mud

Puddle patterns

For those of you who already work with young children, you'll know that most, if not all, love water. It is such a versatile medium, and whether it's from a hose, a tap or natural water source, such as collected rain or puddles, children love splashing, jumping, emptying and filling containers and watching as it moves and changes.

Water in puddles is great because there is a world of possibilities depending on the child's ideas. Some children jump straight in whilst others prefer to sit and watch as the water moves or ripples when hit by dropped stones.

DOI: 10.4324/9781003271710-16

Puddle patterns are just that – patterns that can be seen in puddles. It is exactly what is says on the tin, but taking the time to notice them is where the magic happens. The child who drops rocks and watches the circular motions ripple through the puddle or the mud sitting idle underneath crystal-clear water that, when touched, transforms into almost cloudlike smoke underwater. Depending on the age of the child, observing the patterns can take different forms, and even if you don't have puddles, large containers can be used to drop pebbles in.

Children can also explore schematic concepts here, too. Children who love to throw can happily drop rocks or pebbles into puddles without the worry of being reprimanded as may be the case indoors. The child who likes to get in will love jumping in and out of the puddle repeatedly.

How-to

For this invitation, there is really no prep needed at all (except perhaps a rainy day).

Patterns work best when children can see them, so find a puddle large enough that children can enjoy following their own agenda. It may be useful to find a cluster of puddles so that whilst one child jumps and splashes, another child can sit and observe. It is

important to follow the children's interest and let them guide the play. If appropriate, as described subsequently, you can add to their explorations if they need it, but be mindful about interfering in what may already be creativity at its best.

Top tips

■ Try and go out after the rain has stopped and the puddles have settled. Whilst the rain is a fantastic opportunity and provides the chance to watch the raindrops ripple the water, there is a different opportunity when puddles are calm and waiting for children to explore them.

■ For 2-year-olds, language is the key. Take their lead and comment on what they are doing rather than lead their play. Point out shapes and use language centred around sizes of puddles or water words, such as *drop, plop, drip.*

■ For 3-year-olds, focus again on their ideas but encourage their thinking by asking open-ended questions; ask them to tell you what they see, what they think happens when the rain stops, if they touch the water, how does it feel? If they don't have the language to respond, give them time to think about it and then comment, perhaps asking them to repeat the words.

■ For 4-year-olds, take their lead. Many will share their own thoughts but if they are hesitant, encourage them to touch the water and watch what happens. Ask them to describe how the water is moving and what they can see.

For all children, you can introduce a narrative into their puddle play, too, imagining underwater worlds or creatures who live there.

Remember water; even a few centimetres deep can be dangerous. Never leave children alone near water, and closely supervise young children.

Collections in nature – inspired by the forest approach (Wendy Hamley)

Collecting things is a favourite pastime of many children and can be seen in a number of schema. Children of all ages love to collect and transport items, filling their pockets and showing their friends what they have found. This is a great activity to encourage children's mathematical skills in sorting, categorising and simply having fun exploring what they can find out and about.

How-to

Use some recycled cardboard either in squares or strips (or any shape you'd prefer – you could even ask the children) and wrap string, wool or rubber bands around the card. This will provide a way for the collection to stay on the cardboard once it has been collected.

Go on a walk either in your outdoor area or locally and ask the children to collect anything they think is interesting or they'd like to research or investigate. Have the children add their found objects to their card by weaving them underneath the string or bands, keeping them in place. These can then be displayed as they are by hanging them in the outdoor area or reception areas for parents to see.

Top tips

- Have the card ready for when children need them; we know that children, particularly toddlers, don't wait – by having the card prepped and threaded with string already, children will be able to get straight to collecting.

■ As a variation, you could ask the children (if they are able) to draw a vase or container on their card and poke holes in it rather than thread string. Children can then go out and collect a particular flower for their vase (dandelions and daisies are usually in abundance) and push them through the holes. This is great for pre-school children and the development of fine motor skills; even toddlers will love the challenge of getting the flowers through the holes.

■ Collections can be similar objects or a variety; the beauty of the cardboard bases are they provide a great opportunity for the children to thread their finds. For older children, introducing characteristics to look out for adds another element to searching within nature. With a little bit of preparation, practitioners could provide each child with a ball of clay and a skewer or wooden dowel and collect a certain colour of leaves. The children can create their own rainbows or collections of colours. This also supports their fine motor skills and language development.

(If opting for collections on skewers or wooden dowels, supervise children and be mindful of the edges with younger children – as with all the invitations and suggestions here, you know your children best; risk assess and trust your judgement.)

Large-scale painting

Painting with young children is one of my favourite invitations, and the bigger the better. There is something about large-scale painting that brings an element of freedom children simply can't experience with tabletop creations. Naturally, 2- and 3-year-olds are exploring the world in a very physical way, and large muscle movements can be developed through providing a range of tools for painting, rather than traditional paintbrushes.

There should be no pre-conceived ideas about how the art will turn out, and children should have the freedom to choose their own colours and ways to do things alongside mindful, trusting adults. In an indoor environment, there may be fewer opportunities for complete autonomy as some staff worry about carpet areas, touching resources or the practical downsides to painting indoors. There are ways to manage indoor large-scale activities; however, in this example, outdoors is advised. Whether that is in your outdoor area or a local park or open space, there are less restraints on children and staff through being outdoors; they feel calmer and more at ease about the mess that will inevitably be created.

How-to

There are several ways that large-scale painting can occur outside with a number of different materials that can be used, so the simple how-to here is to ask, what do your children need?

■ Cover a large space with a paper roll, a fabric sheet or large cardboard, and ensure there is enough paint for every child to have a go. It's a great idea to have some paint on standby, too, as when it runs out, they can easily get some more.

■ Add bottles to the area, if you use ready-mixed paint, will enable you to ration the paint to reduce waste (although we have seen that a child's need to use to excess should be facilitated on some occasions). If you have powder paint, why not add small pots of different colours and spray bottles of water for the children to make their own paint. This is great for a range of physical skills but also promotes independence.

■ You will need to consider how you will clean up afterwards. The best way to make sure this happens effectively is to ensure that you are prepared with buckets for the children to wash their hands and that they can easily be changed if needed. There is nothing worse than a group of tired painted children who need to be cleaned all at the same time. With a little thoughtful planning, communication between colleagues and preparation, this can be avoided, resulting in a magically creative session where children are free to explore and make marks the way they choose.

Top tips

■ Consider using fabric instead of paper; that way, you can display it as a wall hanging or cut out sections for other art-making.

■ Ensure you have covered a large enough area to allow several children to collaborate or choose their own section to paint independently. Ultimately, you know your children and what they need best.

■ Try adding paint rollers to encourage large muscle movements.

■ Have some snack nearby as children who are tired or hungry may want to refuel before going back to their activity.

Water potion play

Water is a versatile resource that can be used in hundreds of invitations. It is easily accessible, and children love to watch in wonder as it does magical things both on its own and when other resources are added. Water is also extremely open-ended as children will use what they have to develop their play without adults.

How-to and top tips

Here, I have combined the how-to and top tips, as where water is concerned, they are almost one and the same. For children who love water, there are no hard and fast rules for setting it up, inviting children to play or trying to get them interested; they will do this naturally.

■ Provide children with a variety of different pots, cups, containers.

■ Ensure there is enough water that children don't run out too quickly, although if there are children who are displaying schematic patterns in their play, don't be surprised when the water is being moved from place to place.

■ Provide novelty in the environment (such as bunches of shop-bought flowers) as well as a range of everyday items that children are familiar with.

■ Introduce some bookish play into your explorations as children will enjoy relating it to what they are doing. *The Tiger Who Came to Tea* could encourage a tea party or *Paddington's Garden* could be facilitated by offering fresh flowers in the area.

■ Consider, why not colour the water, too? Water is fantastic on its own, but adding a drop of colour changes the way children engage with it.

- Consider additions such as foam that can also change the experience, and children will love to observe how it changes the water and adds bubbles.

- Use pipettes, small test tubes and funnels to invite investigation into volume and promotes fine motor skills.

- Purchase water beads cheaply from online marketplaces or garden centres. Children will need supervision if you choose them, but on a sunny day, the way they sparkle adds a real sense of awe and wonder to the experience.

Marvellous mud

The final invitations in this chapter are using another one of my favourite mediums, mud.

Mud has so many beneficial properties and yet is regarded as something that should, for the most part, stay on the ground, outside for the children to explore in wellies. I would like to offer alternatives to this belief, grounded in the knowledge of the wonderful, sensory, learning-rich opportunities that mud provides.

 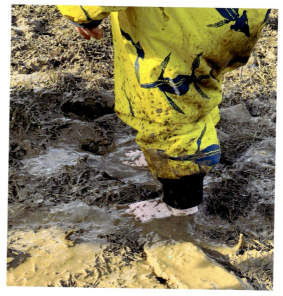

How to practise earthing

- Take children outside and encourage them to come into direct contact with the earth.

- Try this through their hands, feet or whole body.

- Talk to children and comment on how it feels and what it looks like. Ask them to describe it or, if they are not able to, support vocabulary by giving them options and asking them to repeat words.

How to make – mud bricks

■ Gather together some mud, water and flour. Talk to the children about creating a new resource that they can make all by themselves for building towers, bridges and other structures.

■ Start by allowing the children a chance to interact with how the mud feels. They can then start adding flour and water until it resembles a dough.

■ Use bricks as big or as small as you'd like. Ice cubes trays are great for smaller bricks whilst the children can manipulate the dough into squares or rocks for larger bricks.

■ Leave your blocks overnight (they may take a day or two, depending on the water content), and then pop them out of the mould (if you used one).

How to make mud ice desserts

■ These are fantastic to make as an extension to previous mud play opportunities. Once the children have ended their play, ask them to scoop their play residue into moulds. These could be jelly moulds or other cake tins. Try and get at least four or five to ensure they have enough for whatever turn the play takes next.

■ Simply freeze them overnight and pop out of the moulds the next day. Children will be excited to return to their play and explore the added dimension.

How to make a muddy menu

- Consider this another extension to the mud/texture kitchen that you may already provide for children in your setting.

- Add other elements to your play spaces that allow children to be curious learners; this is what early years is all about.

- Have an array of vegetables and natural resources on the table ready for when children come into the play space. This could include sticks, stones, herbs, spices, grasses, carrots, salad leaves, pasta, rice, mud and, of course, a little water.

- Offer alongside saucepans, plates, dessert cups and bowls; children can then revisit narratives supported by the adults who work with them.

References

Abulof, U. (2017) Why We Need Maslow in the Twenty-First Century. *Society*, 54, 508.

Baer, J. (1993) *Creativity and Divergent Thinking: A Task-Specific Approach* (1st ed.). New York: Psychology Press. https://doi.org/10.4324/9781315806785

Berthelsen, D., & Brownlee, J. (2005) Respecting Children's Agency for Learning and Rights to Participation in Child Care Programs. *International Journal of Early Childhood*, 37, 4–5.

Boden, M. (1999) Computer Models of Creativity. In R. J. Sternberg (ed.) *Handbook of Creativity*. Cambridge: Cambridge University Press. pp. 351–372.

Bottrill, G. (2018) *Can I Go and Play Now?* London: SAGE Publications.

Bronfenbrenner, U. (1995) Developmental Psychology Through Space and Time: A Future Perspective. In P. Moen, G. H. Elder, Jr., & K. Luscher (eds.) *Examining Lives in Context: Perspectives on the Ecology of Human Development*. Washington DC: American Psychological Association.

Clark, A., & Moss, P. (2005) *Spaces to Play: More Listening to Young Children Using the Mosaic Approach*. London: National Children's Bureau.

Clark, A., & Moss, P. (2011) *Listening to Young Children. The Mosaic Approach* (2nd ed.). London: National Children's Bureau.

Conkbayir, M. (2020) *Self-Regulation in Early Years, Written January 20th 2020*. Articles – The Foundation Stage Forum (FSF) – Home of Early Years Foundation Stage (eyfs.info) (Accessed 25th April 2022).

Craft, A. (2002) *Creativity and Early Years Education: A Lifewide Foundation*. London: Continuum.

Department for Education (DfE) (2014) *Statutory Framework for the Early Years Foundation Stage*. Available at https://www.gov.uk/government/publications/early-years-foundation-stage-framework--2 (Accessed 8th January 2021).

Department for Education and Skills (DfES) (1999) *All Our Futures*. London: National Advisory Committee on Creative and Cultural Education.

Duffy, B. (2006) *Supporting Creativity and Imagination in the Early Years*. Oxford: Open University Press.

Edwards, C. (2002) Three Approaches from Europe: Waldorf, Montessori and Reggio Emilia. *Early Childhood Research and Practice*, 4, 1–17.

Fisher, J. (2016) *Interacting or Interfering? Improving Interactions in the Early Years*. Berkshire: Open University Press.

Fumoto, H., Robson, S., Greenfield, S., & Hargreaves, D. (2012) *Young Children's Creative Thinking*. London: SAGE Publications.

Glaveanu, V. (2021) *Creativity, a Very Short Introduction*. Oxford: Oxford University Press.

Graue, M. E., & Walsh, D. J. (1998) *Studying Children in Context: Theories, Methods, and Ethics*. London: SAGE Publications.

Greenman, J., & Stonehouse, A. (1996) *Prime Times: A Handbook for Excellence in Infant Toddler Programs*. St. Paul, MN: Redleaf Press.

Gross, R. D., & Humphreys, P. (1992) *Psychology: The Science of Mind and Behavior*. London: Hodder & Stoughton.

Hanscom, A. (2016) *Balanced and Barefoot*. Oakland, CA: New Harbinger Publications.

Haughey, S. (2020) *Wonder Art Workshop*. Beverly, MA: Quatro Publishing Group PLC.

Hedegaard, M., & Fleer, M. (2013) *Play, Learning, and Children's Development: Everyday Life in Families and Transition to School*. Cambridge: Cambridge University Press.

Hirst, K., & Nutbrown, C. (2005) *Perspectives on Early Childhood Education*. Staffordshire, England: Trentham Books.

Isaacs, S. (1929) *The Nursery Years*. London: Routledge.

Johnson, J., & Watts, A. (2019) *Developing Creativity and Curiosity Outdoors: How to Extend Creative Learning in the Early Years*. London: Routledge.

Johnson-Laird, P. N. (1988) Freedom and Constraint in Creativity. In R. J. Sternberg (ed.) *The Nature of Creativity: Contemporary Psychological Perspectives*. Cambridge: Cambridge University Press. pp. 202–217.

Jones, P. (2009) *Rethinking Childhood: Attitudes in Contemporary Society*. London: Continuum.

Kaufman, J. C., & Sternberg, R. J. (2007) Resource Review: Creativity. *Change*, 39, 55–58.

Keenan, T., & Evans, S. (2009) *An Introduction to Child Development* (2nd ed.). London: SAGE Publications.

Laevers, F. (2005) The Curriculum as Means to Raise the Quality of ECE. Implications for Policy. *European Early Childhood Education Research Journal*, 13, 17–30.

Langston, A., & Abbott, L. (2004) Quality Matters. In L. Abbott & A. Langston (eds.) *Birth to Three Matters*. Maidenhead: Open University Press.

Lee, T. (2016) *Princesses, Dragons and Helicopter Stories; Storytelling and Story Acting in the Early Years*. Oxon: Routledge.

Longstaffe, M. (2020) *Provocations for Learning in Early Years Settings. A Practical Guide*. London: Jessica Kingsley Publishers.

Manning-Morton, J., & Thorp, M. (2015) *Two-Year Olds in Early Years Settings*. Berkshire: Open University Press.

Mashford-Scott A., & Church, A. (2011) Promoting Children's Agency in Early Childhood Education, Novitas-ROYAL. *Research on Youth and Language*, 5(1), 15–38.

Mashford-Scott, A., Church, A., & Tayler, C. (2012) Seeking Children's Perspectives on Their Wellbeing in Early Childhood Settings. *International Journal of Early Childhood*, 44(3), 231–247.

May, P. (2009) *Creative Development in the Early Years Foundation Stage*. Oxon: Routledge

Meador, K. S. (1992) Emerging Rainbows: A Review of the Literature on Creativity. *Journal for the Education of the Gifted*, 15(2), 163–181.

Meadows, S. (2006) *The Child as Thinker: The Development and Acquisition of Cognition in Childhood*. London: Routledge.

Moga, E., Burger, K., Hetland, L., & Winner, E. (2000) Does Studying the Arts Engender Creative Thinking? Evidence for Near But Not Far Transfer. *Journal of Aesthetic Education*, 34(3/4), 91–104. https://doi.org/10.2307/3333639

Mohammed, R. (2018) *Creative Learning in the Early Years: Nurturing the Characteristics of Creativity*. Oxon: Routledge.

Montessori, M. (1982 [1949]) *The Absorbent Mind* (8th ed.). Madras, India: Kalakshetra Publications.

Moorhouse, P. (2018) *Learning Through Woodwork; Introducing Creative Woodwork in the Early Years*. London: Routledge.

National Advisory Committee on Creative and Cultural Education (1999) *All Our Futures: Creativity, Culture and Education*. London: DFEE.

Nicholson, E. (2005) The School Building as Third Teacher. In M. Dudek (ed.) *Children's Spaces*. London: Architectural Press.

Oldfield, L. (2001) *Free to Learn; Introducing Steiner Waldorf Early Education*. Gloucestershire: Hawthorn Press.

Pascal, C., & Bertram, T. (2009) Listening to Young Citizens: The Struggle to Make a Real Participatory Paradigm in Research With Young Children. *European Early Childhood Education Research Journal*, 17, 249–262.

Pascal, C., & Bertram, T. (2017) *Creativity and Critical Thinking Are Central to an effective Early Years Curriculum and Pedagogy*. BECERA. Available at www.becera.org.uk

Pikler, E. (1979) The Competence of an Infant. *The Pikler Collection*. Available at https://thepiklercol-lection.weebly. com/uploads/9/4/5/3/9453622/the_competence_of_and_infant_full_-_pikler.pdf (Accessed February 2021)

Pound, L. (2011) *Influencing Early Childhood Education*. Berkshire: Open University Press.

Rogoff, B. (2003) *The Cultural Nature of Human Development*. Oxford and New York: Oxford University Press.

Sharp, C. (2004) Developing Young Children's Creativity: What Can We Learn From Research? *Readership Primary*, 32.

Slade, M., Lowery, C., & Bland, K. (2013) Evaluating the Impact of Forest Schools: A Collaboration Between a University and a Primary School. *British Journal of Learning Support*, 28(2), 66–72.

Vygotsky, L. S. (1988) The Genesis of Higher Mental Functions. In K. Richardson & S. Sheldon (eds.) *Cognitive Development to Adolescence*. Hove, Sussex: Elbaum.

Winnicott, D. W. (2005) *Playing and Reality*. London: Routledge Classics.

Index